To Judy —
A terrific!
Who inspired
write this book. I
am ever so grateful!
much love,

Craig

Phil. 4:4
11-2-15

A

Faith

For All

Seasons

Craig M. Kallio

For my wife Pamela....
who lives the gospel every day.

A Faith for All Seasons

Printed in the United States

First Printing by Amazon

CONTENT

ADVENT

CHRISTMAS

EPIPHANY

CONTENT

LENT

EASTER

PENTECOST

Advent

ADVENT SPEAKS TO OUR DEEPEST LONGINGS

Isaiah 40:1-5

Each year as we anticipate the Advent season we like to believe this will be the year our piety gets once-and-for-all in sync with a genuine sense of what Advent is really about, a notion which for numerous reasons has alluded us up to this stage of our maturing faith.

As the busyness of our lives contained within the four weeks of Advent begins to capture more and more of our time and energy, we often hear the phrase, "Here we go again." The words and how they're said are often an expression of the excitement and anticipation we get caught up in as we look forward to Christmas and the accompanying gift giving. Other times they betray a dread of holiday crowds, power shopping, and congested traffic. But, as is often the case, whenever we hear a reference to something happening *again*, our mind references an event or history repeating itself. This repeating sense of time and history, as we inevitably discover, has its origin in Greek thought which sees the same patterns endlessly repeating themselves over and over again. This sense of history is implied by George Santayana's statement that those who do not learn the lessons of history are doomed to repeat them.

Beginning in chapter 40 of Isaiah's prophecy the writer approaches the concepts of time and history in a manner we would today describe as "linear." According to this view, the normal course of events is interpreted by new events rather than being predicated on the basis of the old. Linear history disrupts the ordinary passage of time and instead begins new patterns in our lives. For example, when we say Advent is coming again we are referencing past experiences of Advent in order to characterize our expectations for Advent *this* year. We use the past to define the present, and then we proceed to live into it. The result is what is referred to as cyclical history. Mike Royko, who for years wrote for the Chicago Sun Times, once described cyclical history as "The same [darn] thing all over again."

As Isaiah describes it, in a foreign land, among a foreign people, deprived of temple and accompanying sacrifices, their sacred vessels in the hands of pagans, the Jews sat down and wept. This was their second great captivity. Just as they were slaves in Egypt, they became resident aliens in Babylon longing for freedom and home. Isaiah speaks to their waning hope: "*Comfort, O comfort my people says your God. Speak tenderly to Jerusalem*" (40:1, RSV). They are summoned to work out their salvation in a forward-thinking manner, discerning what God would gradually unfold before them. Isaiah continues with this directive, "*In the wilderness prepare the way of the Lord, make straight in the desert a highway for our God*" (vs. 43). Let's face it, we can only make straight that which is before us, not behind us. Theirs was to be a new vision of hope as the breath of the Lord makes its way over the face of the earth in order to restore their soul as well as their identity. The prophet's words are reminiscent of what would be heard much later in the biblical narrative from John the Baptist, a wild voice that howls in the wilderness.

One factor that would distinguish Isaiah's message from our hearing it today is the fact that Isaiah's audience was made up of people who knew their need for comfort as well as their need for God. As a nation they longed to relegate to their past the dark powers of the world's wilderness. But then, are we any different? We all long for comfort. None of us is completely unhitched from the fear of being lost and anxious. The wilderness is no stranger to us because it resides inside us. Our wilderness is personal; it knows our name. It is losing a parent or child or a spouse to death or estrangement. It is living with the disease of depression or addiction or with chronic pain and illness. It is aging and loneliness. It is seeing our children's families splinter and break up. It is the feeling of powerlessness and agony as we lose our grandchildren to divorce. For others it may be retirement that has fallen flat for lack of direction, meaning, and purpose. For others it may be less specific, but painful nonetheless. There isn't anyone among us who is so sheltered and privileged as to not be touched or affected by the wilderness of the world in some way.

What made God's words of prophecy so astonishing was that the prophet Isaiah himself was plagued with doubt and despair. His message of hope was delivered despite his own hopelessness. Add to that the fact that the people to whom the message was delivered were themselves hopeless. Think about it. The prospects for returning to their homeland were nil. By every rational measurement, the promise of God seemed quite impossible. But that's the way it is with this God we worship, a God who delights in doing impossible things.

When God comes the world will not stay the same; according to Isaiah's words valleys shall rise, rough ground will smooth out, jagged mountains will be leveled. Yes, those are Isaiah's own words. The message he is given to announce is one of hope and promise, *"Prepare the way of the Lord."* They couldn't be any clearer. The coming of God will not be business as usual, nor does God's comfort imply more of the same in our lives. God comes *anew*, not *again*, and the world will never be as it was before. Our ultimate hope and trust are in the God who comes to make us new and to give us comfort in our newness.

We who know the feeling of exile often think we need a God of massive strength to save us from the fear that erupts within us in those dark times. I remember my first Christmas as a priest, newly called to a downtown parish and my family 80 miles away, not yet having moved. Being alone I made myself available in the hours before the Christmas Eve Mass should anyone wish to stop by the church to make their confession or just to talk. This is when I met Robert for the first time. He told me of his attendance at every Christmas Eve service for the past ten years. When I inquired about the years which preceded his church attendance he proceeded to tell me a most unforgettable story.

Immediately prior to his coming to church he told me how his life had imploded on him. A long-term relationship had come to an abrupt end. Within the past eighteen months his parents had passed on. Life, he said, had grown stale, and even his job, which by this time had begun to feel more like the vocation he longed for, began to lose its luster. His indifference poured over into depression which quickly advanced to excessive drinking, which in-turn eventually delivered him within sight of death's door. It was a chance encounter with a server at a restaurant that turned on a light in his mind. The server was wondering where he might go to find a Christmas Eve service. This brought Robert back to his own childhood when, as a tradition, he would accompany his family to the Christmas Eve service. Perhaps, he thought, this server's inquiry was a providential moment that would connect his memory of church with an actual decision to go to church that evening. It filled a long-empty void that nothing else he had ever tried could ever accomplish. More than this, though, it brought birth to a journey of exploration that would transform a long-dormant faith which would proceed to ferry him out of his wilderness towards a life which provided a generous dose of meaning, purpose, and hope.

Looking back on this it is possible to recognize the linear nature of what happened here. The normal course of events he could now see through a different lens, one which saw his life's shape and meaning take their direction from new events, rather than old ones played over again. For Robert that evening service was "Christmas anew" rather than "Christmas again."

For us to experience such a reversal in our own lives is to embody a spirit of readiness, expectancy, the softening of a hardened heart, the tuning of the mind to a new revelation instead of "more of the same." But this is a conscious decision we must make for ourselves and now in Advent is a good time to make it. *"Comfort, O comfort my people, says your God."* These are words for those of us who always seem to have at least one foot in the wilderness and who need to know the kind of life where God is always a present reality. A life that not only longs for God, but is all bound up in God's purposes and hope for us all. A life where we welcome with open and expectant arms that which Advent points us toward: our journey to the manger *anew,* not the manger *again.*

ANTIDOTE FOR A RESTLESS HEART

Matthew 11:1-10

It is human nature to be restless in our encounters with life in general. St. Augustine begins his brilliant work, *Confessions*, by reminding us that "Our hearts are restless until they find their rest in Thee, O God." But we are also a people in pursuit of something bigger, better, and more exciting. The eleventh chapter of Matthew's Gospel begins with a statement that sounds awfully strange. It is even more so when we discover it comes from the lips of John the Baptist. We wonder if John isn't struggling with his own restless heart when he asks, *"Are you the One?"* He is referencing none other than Jesus. Could his angst have anything to do with the enormity of the clout Jesus would inflict on Herod's realm or is it about Jesus' Divinity? Currently locked away in Herod's prison, the once free, desert roaming John the Baptist can now only proclaim his message to the lifeless, response-less walls that surround him, or to his cellmates.

We look at ourselves and ask if this is really who I want to be? Is this how I want to live? Sometimes, being in that boxed-in, caught-in-the-treadmill place becomes a place of transformation. It doesn't take much imagination to recognize that our culture is filled with boxed-in, locked-up places. There is a stark difference between John in Herod's dungeon and us in twenty-first century America. There is no doubt in John's mind that he is a prisoner. Unlike us, John does not suffer under the illusion that he is going to somehow mastermind his own emancipation. He knows there is no freedom inside Herod's jail, no matter what face he tries to put on it. He doesn't look towards the day when he finally adapts to prison life. John knows that another world exists, that there is another way out. *"When John heard in prison what the Messiah was doing, he sent word by his disciples, and said to him, 'Are you the one who is to come, or are we to wait for another'"* (11:3).

- 5 -

John's question is our question. But, unlike John, we are not cognizant of the fact that we are in prison. The bars and doors of our prison are not Herod's penitentiary, and yet they are just as real, and just as binding. For most of us, we have a hard time seeing our "prisons" for what they are. We've been imprisoned for so long we have forgotten what freedom outside the walls really is, and as a result we have adapted our lives if only to make our conditions better behind bars rather than opting for the more challenging choice of complete release. The things we are addicted to provide us with a good example. It's not just the obvious ones like alcohol and illicit drugs, but there's also our addiction to "things" like the latest clothing fashion, the newest and fanciest automobile, even silly little rituals that either play out in our minds or unravel before our own eyes. We who are in denial recognize our names on many of them that cross our paths in the course of a lifetime. They may be minor, but they are nevertheless the real thing.

Being in prison, though, does offer the opportunity to look at the world from a new perspective with boxed-in, locked-up places. No matter how adept we think we are at avoiding the many traps occasioned along our way, we will all do our time, one way or another. Jesus' response to John's troubling question could have been thrown back at John: "What were *you* looking for?"

John the Baptist in the bowels of Herod's jail is the prototype of Advent hope. He lives in the lightless world between what is and what is hoped for. It could be said he is looking for a Deliverance---for himself and Israel. The placement of this text in Advent is a reminder that now is the time to come to terms with our need and craving for emancipation, no matter how "together" we seem and appear to the world. C.S. Lewis said, "Every story of conversion is the story of a blessed defeat," and in this experience of disorientation-meeting-the-Gospel, reorientation blessedly occurs. In our world today we are the ones who are blessed by defeat to look beyond self-management and over-control to imagine something different.

Here we would expect Jesus to offer John an answer. But he doesn't. While Jesus stays clear of telling John authoritatively and decisively, "I am the Messiah," he does something else that is exceedingly more worthwhile, even if John doesn't yet recognize it. Jesus invites John to consider what his followers can *see and hear.* It is as if he were saying "Look around you," because it is only in the encounter with Jesus---as well as the experience of his power to release and restore---that we come to deep faith. So Jesus is really asking "What more do you want?" His words implore them to open their eyes because only then will they will see the signs and wonders of God bubbling up all around them. It is in such moments when we followers of Jesus fail to recognize such stellar manifestations of God's power that we begin to wonder if perhaps somebody else is doing a better job in mission and ministry than we are, or if God's healing work is more present in other churches than our own. We might even convince ourselves that if we go to a different church we will find something bigger, better, and more exciting. Added to that assumption is our belief that going to where the conditions are "just right" is where we will certainly find the happiness that has eluded us.

I recently came upon a book by author Kent Nerburn entitled *Small Graces* in which he talks about life being transient, lived on the run, characterized by its endless sense of movement which, he says, is akin to chasing the future. As a result, he maintains, "We seldom pause to shine a light upon the ordinary moments, to hallow them with our own attentiveness, to honor them with gentle caring." Nerburn's remedy is for us "to find ways to lift the moments of our daily lives---to celebrate and consecrate the ordinary." He invites us, as a result, to see the world with fresh eyes, reminding us that "though we may not live a holy life, we live in a world alive with holy moments" (New World Library, 1998).

Whatever disillusionment John the Baptist experiences, he does not renounce Jesus. His issue with doubt grows out of God's apparent failure to meet the expectations he has set for himself, a hint of which we see when John preaches the coming of the one who "*will baptize with the Holy Spirit and fire. His winnowing fork in his hand"* as he prepares to separate wheat from chaff in holy conflagration (Matthew 3:11c-12). John wants his doubts answered with judgment, but Jesus said his purpose was redemption and grace. Jesus is not going to overcome Herod's tyranny in the manner of a conquering King David nor match Herod's violence with his own style of vengeance. There are many of us today who still want our doubts answered by judgment, and yet I find it strange how grace seems to be what always works to transform our hearts and minds. Jesus does not come to fulfill our expectations but to overturn them. If we begin looking for the kingdom in light of our own needs, our own preconceived ideas, our own expectations, we will, like John, always live in doubt and miss the real truth about Jesus.

Jesus' advice transmitted back to John couldn't be any clearer. *"Go and tell John what you hear and see. The blind receive their sight, the lame walk, the lepers are cleansed, the deaf hear, the dead are raised, and the poor have good news brought to them"* (11:4-6). One hopes John, in the darkness of his cell shadowed by his faltering faith, came to a place of peace which, inherent in the testimony of Jesus delivered to him, surpasses understanding. In his dungeon, John, reaching out to "the one who is to come," experiences the beginning of faith: God's deliverance rightly understood in Jesus, the Hope of Advent, indeed, the hope of all our Advents.

What has always been precious and uplifting to me from the writings of G.K. Chesterton is when he said, "it is only when everything is hopeless that hope begins to be a strength at all. Like all Christian virtues, it is unreasonable as it is indispensable." This tossed together mixture of doubt and uncertainty hardly seems the way to celebrate the season. But then, will we ever truly understand Jesus' intrusion into our conventional Christmas?

WHAT SHALL WE DO?

Philippians 4:1-7 and Luke 3:7-18

The celebration of the Season of Advent is not meant to be a sort of mini-Lent, born as an off-shoot of Lent. And yet Advent does embody some of the trappings of Lent. Central, of course, is our need for introspection as reflected in John the Baptist's call to repent, *"You brood of vipers! Who warned you to flee the wrath to come?"* (Luke 3:7b). Advent, though, does allow for rejoicing, a time of lightness in a season of penitence. Such was the spirit of Paul in his proclamation, *"Rejoice in the Lord always; again I say rejoice"* (v. 4). But the type of rejoicing that we embody in Advent is not a joy that ignores the harsh realities of life. Instead, it is a joy that is based on our ability to recognize God's love and presence in our lives. This enablement comes despite the chasm that is nevertheless present between God's cherished hopes and intentions for us and the reality of how we actually live our lives one day to the next. It is a joy that comes to us in the wilderness and times of our deepest darkness.

One such veil that often plagues us comes from the mind of Oscar Wilde when he commented on how he identifies agitators as being nothing less than "a set of interfering, meddling people who come down to some perfectly contented community and sow the seeds of discontent among them." Which is why, surprisingly, he concludes, "agitators are so absolutely necessary." In the case of John the Baptist's ranting, he doesn't confront simply to be obnoxious. He confronts because he knows that rarely do people change until they experience some sort of "judgment." Wrongly understood as "condemnation," prophetic judgment is a call to change. It is the call to get out of denial. None of those in the crowd ask John what they should *think*. They ask *"What shall we do."* The desert preacher addresses the crowd, tax collectors, and soldiers, with an uncompromising demand for fairness and justice. Generosity and unselfishness are the proper "fruit" of repentance. John tells them in no uncertain terms that if they really want to be prepared for what is to come, if they really want to be baptized, *then* provide evidence of a repentant heart! John's challenge to them is nothing less than a mental and spiritual U-turn.

For John, repentance has less to do with how fervently one prays or how faithfully one attends church. Rather, it is a call to bring back together what in today's vernacular we call religion and ethics. At the time of the corporate collapse of business giant Enron as the result of an enormous corruption scandal several years ago, observers noted how some in upper management, including the top executive, were frequent church-goers, which brings to mind the phrase "right worship and right actions." The former without the latter does little good for the world. The latter without the former results in a dry, depressing moralism. When Desmond Tutu was the Bishop of Johannesburg, before becoming Archbishop of South Africa, he would tell his audiences a particular story without the slightest hint of bitterness, but rather a spirit of humility. "When the missionaries first came to Africa, they had the Bible and we had the land. They said, 'Let us pray.' We closed our eyes. When we opened them, the tables had been turned. We had the Bible, and they had the land."

Humility, conceivably a by-product of repentance, is often the leaven of ministry. As Christians, we espouse the virtue of humility, often forgetting that the path to humility is painful because it involves debunking our deepest and most cherished illusions. The virtue of humility has always been an important attribute of any Christian journey and is no less important in ministering to others. Humility, like doubt, undercuts our self-certainties, our tendency to believe we know what's best for others, our self-righteous pieties, and our desire to share life or serve only those who agree with our cherished beliefs, biases, and perhaps even our expectations. Experts tell us that the pain of humility, when accepted, creates a space for us to see ourselves and others more clearly, and, more importantly, is a necessary step in developing our capacity for empathy and compassion, virtues for which Desmond Tutu has centered his life and ministry around.

Sometimes I can't contain my own resentments about the manner in which John the Baptist intrudes upon the loveliness of this festive season, "*The voice of one crying in the wilderness.*" He's a square peg for the round holes in our Advent calendars. On the heels of John's howling diatribe, Luke brings it to its conclusion with, "*So, with many other exhortations, he proclaimed the good news to the people*" (v. 18). Was John's message really good news? Perhaps, if we can find it within ourselves to answer yes to a few questions..

In the first place, John's message is good news if we *expect* change. Luke reminds us, "*The people were filled with expectation*" (v. 15). Why wouldn't they expect change? They were watching for something they weren't even sure they could recognize if they saw it. They were waiting, though they didn't know just what would happen or when. Lacking such a mind-set, John's words strike us like piercing static interrupting a beautiful Christmas carol.

Secondly, his message can come across as good news if we are *willing* to change. It was too much to ask of the Pharisees and the Sadducees, as far as Luke's story goes. He leaves them out entirely even though it's probable they were within earshot of John the Baptist. Luke probably wonders how they could have heard John's message and then declined to enter the new era in which God is visibly in charge. Luke can't picture the ones who plotted against Jesus and crucified him as people who were influenced in any way by John's preaching.

Finally, though, to *actually change*, which is what happened to the people who heard Peter preach at Pentecost; when the Holy Spirit came like the sound of rushing wind "*were cut to the heart and said to Peter and to the other apostles, 'Brothers, what should we do?'*" (Acts 22:10). And after an earthquake shook the foundation of the Philippian jail so hard that the gates flew wide open and everyone's chains came unfastened, the trembling jailer, prevented by Paul from committing suicide because he had failed as a jailer, asked, "*Sirs, what must I do to be saved?*" (Acts 6:30). In the same way, it wasn't too much to ask of the common people that they be willing to change. When they heard the powerful appeal of John, they began asking, "*What*, then, shall we do?" In John's mind, by simply sharing their food and clothing with those who had none would satisfy them with the power to change.

How would John's sermon shine a spotlight on the contemporary church today? We church-going people can't appeal to our ancestry, our affiliations, or our achievements, even as grand as they might be. But if we expect the Savior's coming to change our life, we will hear in this good news the summons to a way of being, an integrity of action, memory, and identity that is not only compelling, but can even be comforting and reassuring. It is a call back to the life we claimed when we passed through the baptismal waters, uniting the church in a covenant of integrity, self-reflection, and openness to the One who puts us in our Advent hope. Perhaps then the message of John the Baptist will find a happy place on our Advent calendar, and from this time forward we will understand why Luke recognized the significance of the desert prophet's words enough to be written down for future generations, "*He proclaimed good news to the people.*"

ADVENT AS A DESTINY

Luke 3:1-6

In his book, *The Abolition of Man*, C.S. Lewis points out that "For the wise man of old, the cardinal problem of human life was how to conform the soul to objective reality, and the solution was wisdom, self-discipline, and virtue. For the modern, the cardinal problem is how to conform reality to the wishes of man, and the solution is technique."

As a part of our Advent discipline, when we look around and take stock of how life is these days, what grabs us most is the sense of being unsettled. It seems as though our technique may not be working. We may be asking ourselves where are the prophets who will set us on a path toward meaning and unconditional joy. As a child I lived with an innate suspicion of Advent. In my young and impressionable mind the yearly observance of Advent felt not at all like the expectation of the ancient people I studied about in Sunday school. Theirs was a life of drama, not knowing how, when, or if God's messiah would appear. Our household, on the other hand, knew precisely how Advent would end. In comparison with the ancient Israelites, whatever dramatic tension experienced in our family usually emerged from our shopping.

Yet, at the same time, Advent had its way and infiltrated my heart. I have matured much since then and have come to understand how a child can often grasp the reality of what I call *eager expectation*, and experience the ensuing joy far better than we adults. Something about the anticipation wafting above our imaginative minds mixed in with the cold and darkness outside--- when contrasted alongside the candles, solemnity and warmth indoors---made the Advent drama real; the invisible God taking on our flesh and becoming a visible actor on the stage of the universe.

The author Luke doesn't bring John the Baptist onto the biblical stage by describing any sort of "technique." Rather, the author borrows from the prophet Isaiah with words that would echo throughout the Jordan valley centuries later from John the Baptist, *"Prepare the way of the Lord, make his paths straight"* (v. 4b, RSV). To "make straight" in this sense is not about improving upon techniques with a proven track record. John has something much more germane to the people's own sense of expectation, as proclaimed by the ancient prophets. How strange of God to begin the way of Christianity with this untamed, uncivilized man. John was an ascetic, and as such had little desire to "win friends and influence people." He could care less about taking polls or making decisions based on what he says. In the simplest, most practical way John the Baptist sets his sights on addressing the inequities prevalent in society and the greed that feeds those inequities. The mantra is for the pathways to be straight, he reminds them.

That innocent-sounding phrase *"...the word of God came to John,"* (v. 2) tucked among the list of the "Who's Who," ought to give us pause whenever we hear it, like when we feel powerless in the face of complex problems of our day. How can little-ole-me possibly make even a dent in solving world hunger. Isn't it up to the economists and agricultural experts to tackle this? How can I begin to influence for Christ a world that appears to care less and less about things religious? And yet, how can we ever forget how throughout history God has shown a preference for the non-experts to take on God's most vital work.

This little phrase, *"the word of God came to John,"* ought to strike a chord when we hear a voice within to get in touch with a friend we haven't seen for a while, or when we feel an inward nudge to tell a loved one just why it is we believe in Christ, or when we sense now is the moment to give our time to the church. We ought to remember the time when instead of any sort of technique, it was something within that nudged, that drove an ordinary man named John to do something he was good at, and, when he did respond, how it made a big difference. This easily overlooked phrase is one that speaks about a great God who uses little people to accomplish larger purposes about which we are deeply concerned. Little people like us.

John the Baptist comes in Advent to remind us that it is in the very middle of human life that faith begins. He is born in the wilderness. His faith is shaped by the wilderness. He may carry the wilderness with him wherever he goes, but today John the Baptist comes out of the wilderness into the mainstream of human life to call us to faith. But he doesn't call us away from our work and responsibilities to join him in the wilderness. Why should he? We have enough wilderness in our own environment, and *that* is where faith begins and where faith is most needed.

We can't escape the fact that Luke begins telling of John the Baptist by locating John's ministry in the historical, political, social, and cultural events of the day: *"In the fifteenth year of the reign of Emperor Tiberius,"* and so on (v. 1). Faith does not begin in some religious fantasy land, nor does it begin in some secluded religious corner of our lives. It begins right here in the mix of events---both sacred and secular---that shape our lives. *"Prepare the way of the Lord"* is what John proclaimed because God is invading ordinary human lives.

This could be the reason why the Advent of my youth awoke me to the disparity between the advent of Christ for the ancient Israelites, and the coming of Christ for us today. That is why Advent belongs to the dissatisfied because Advent, deep down, resonates only to the ill-at-ease. Only the unfulfilled---the ones disquieted by their exiled condition---yearn for a new destination, a new dispensation. Who hears the Word of God in Advent? Who welcomes the vision, who drinks in its hope and promises of salvation?

The playwright, T.S. Eliot, introduced his religious drama, *Murder in the Cathedral*, in Advent. It recounts the circumstances that surrounded the life of Thomas a' Beckett leading up to his being slain in Canterbury Cathedral in 1170. At one point the women of Canterbury are assembled to anticipate the return of Archbishop Beckett from France. The advent Eliot depicts echoes Luke's advent. Both are anxious to emphasize that their advent stories give evidence of God acting in history with real people. John the Baptist is on his way through the regions around Jordan.

Similarly, in the grand chorus which launches Eliot's play, the women of Canterbury proclaim, "Destiny waits in the hand of God, shaping the still unshapen." We, too, have our own advent. Are we preparing the way by our technique, or by way of God's destiny? It is a destiny that shapes all of God's unshapen who await the One who is to come, little people like you and me.

Christmas

CHRISTMAS EVE

Luke 2:1-14

I don't imagine there are many of us who make a habit of watching the same movie over and over again. But in our home there are three particular ones that we make a point of watching year after year. They all happen to be Christmas stories. Though none of them specifically focuses on the birth of Christ, imbedded in each is the theme of thankfulness for having received an unexpected grace.

Why do people watch the same movie over and over again? The plot is the same. Nothing changes. And yet in a similar vein, every Christmas Eve we listen to the same story we heard last year. I know that for me it is good in this unsettled world to have this consistency---the Christmas Eve service. There is holiness to memory, a sense of God's presence in the mangers of the mind. This might explain why it is that the occasions that change the least are often the very occasions that change us the most. The fact that we ourselves change and the circumstances that surround our lives change one year to another---if only minutely---opens us up to those things that stay the same.

German theologian Helmut Thielicke made the observation, "The greatest mysteries of God are always enacted in the depths." Immediately after the end of World War II Thielicke was preaching to his congregation in Stuttgart. As you can imagine, their country was in ruins, and so was their old church. There was no one in attendance who had not lost loved ones, their homes, their means of economic support, and their former way of life. He was teaching on the Lord's Prayer, and when he came to the phrase, "Thy kingdom come," he stopped and asked how these words could have any meaning. He answered his own question by reminding his people, "Before, our lives were safe, happy, and well-ordered. But now we see how deceptive appearances were. Now the telephone wires are down, the hospitals and shops and transportation centers are bombed out. There's no food or medicine. Now there is just us---and God" (source unknown).

While Thielicke's words do not imply that we have to be war-torn people before Christmas sinks deeper than mall madness, it does mean that the Gospel is heard most profoundly where there is no hope of saving ourselves. It is heard where people have tried all sorts and conditions of paths of self-satisfaction only to find themselves beaten down by the world they have sought to master. The Gospel is heard where the path of self-satisfaction has been followed as the way. Where the path of self-mastery and self-absorption have been heralded as the way. And, for a while, these worked. But then the paths ended. Only God remained.

To all of those wearied by trying to save themselves, the prophet Isaiah makes a startling promise this Holy Night. *"The people who walked in the darkness have seen a great light; those who have lived in a land of deep darkness---on them light has shined"* (9:2). The Light has shined and perhaps shined most poignantly on the ones who have bet their lives on all the paths except the Gospel path. These are the ones who are ready to receive the way, the truth, and the life that Christmas declares is born today. Beaten down by the "structure," they are the ones ready for the "anti-structure." They are ready for the Kingdom to come, on earth as in heaven---to come in Jesus.

When we come to church on Christmas Eve we sing songs and tell stories about the joy of coming to the manger and finding the Christ Child. I am reminded of the story of a little girl who wandered off into the forest and became lost. As it grew dark her frantic parents and neighbors scoured the forest calling out her name. Early in the morning, the father came to a clearing and saw where the little girl had lain down to sleep. He ran toward her, and with a great shout of joy she exclaimed, "Daddy, I found you." As we encounter once again this precious newborn tonight, we are reminded of what is central to the Christian faith: The glad and glorious news that we have been found by God. And while we recognize that God acting in our lives is a day-to-day affirmation, we dare not miss the significance between celebrating God's *acting* in the world and God's *entering* the world.

Mary and Joseph made the journey to Bethlehem, navigating the rough terrain, one tiring, terrible step after the other---only to be shut out of a decent place to stay. And *this* child with *these* parents, in *that* situation, will be heralded as "Savior," the "Wonderful Counselor," or the "Prince of Peace." Isn't that absolutely amazing? But that is the resolute message we proclaim each Christmas Eve. It is a brazen, some say prosperous, claim. And rest assured, all interfaith goodwill aside, no other religion will go along with confessing it. No Muslim, or Jew, or Buddhist, or Hindu will affirm what we do tonight. That in Bethlehem's stall of straw surrounded by mute animals, the risk of all risks is taken. The unknowable becomes known. The infinite becomes finite. The Word becomes flesh. God's rescue operation---freeing us and the world from going down all the sorts and conditions of paths that lead us nowhere, really.

Episcopal bishop, John Hines, was fond of telling the story about the traveler who passed through the Louvre without so much as the faintest stirring of interest within him. As he stalked out the door, he said quiet loudly, "There is nothing all that great to see in here." The museum guard standing by the door overheard the remark, and in his quiet manner replied, "Sir, the paintings in here are not on trial. It is the spectators who are." And, similarly, it is not Jesus and the Holy Family who are on trial in the Christmas celebration. We are. Perhaps because we have an inkling this might be true, we come Christmas Eve to hear the story again so that we can be reminded once again how it feels to receive an unexpected grace. Occasions that change the least are very often the occasions that change us the most.

In a Christmas sermon from thirteenth- century mystic Meister Eckhart, he preached about how Christmas is something that happens within us. Again this Christmas we long for God to find us because we know, within us, our human condition of estrangement and lostness and enslavement to sin and death will once again meet the grace and truth that Jesus embodies. Christmas faith is born not just in the Bethlehem manger, but in the lives of those who cannot save themselves and who know this to be true. Blessed are they.

IT WASN'T AN ACCIDENT

Luke 2: [1-7] 8-20

"And it came to pass....." With these simple words taken from the King James Bible, God introduces the greatest miracle of history. The birth of Jesus Christ didn't just happen. It took an eternity of planning. Echoing through the corridors of Old Testament time was the voice of God in prophecy foretelling the coming Messiah. And then---after an eternity of planning and centuries of promising---he faithfully kept his word. God's plan of salvation is an inclusive one which includes Caesars, shepherds, innkeepers, census-takers, and angels. Each was God-picked for a role in the unfolding drama. It is not only the miracle of birth, but also the divinity of life just as God planned it. Through his life comes God's abundance. Madeleine L'Engle puts it this way. "This is the irrational season when love blooms bright and wild. Had Mary ben filled with reason there'd have been no room for the child" (*The Irrational Season*, p. 27).

Underscoring the irrationality of this season is the often overlooked pivotal role God gives to the arch-nemesis, a historical convergence in which the promise of God through Scripture comes true because of an enactment of the Roman authorities. The purposes of God unfold not only through the doubt of Zechariah and the exuberance of Elizabeth, not just through the visitations of the archangel Gabriel and the model trust of Mary, but also through the unwitting Caesar Augustus. Such anomalies are also scattered throughout our own past. For example, history has shown how a great deal of the world's beauty is born in hidden places, how a surprising number of our most significant scientific discoveries---penicillin and uranium---emerge in unlikely places, and how many financial empires begin in garages and back rooms, which is why we dare not write off the significant small things.

Because the story of our Lord's birth is a familiar one, we need to be careful in how we approach it again this year. If we assume we know everything there is to know about it, and have convinced ourselves we have gleaned every ounce of meaning from it, we will most assuredly miss God's message for us this Christmas. But the question we come to address each year at this time is the allure and the attraction over the birth of *this* child. It may be that the seemingly mystical power in the telling of the story every Christmas is the way it humbles us, stripping away the pretensions of culture and civilization, the trappings of wealth and ease and comfort. The vision of God in a manger turns all of that upside down. It makes the last first; it pulls down the pride of the powerful; it disarms the wisdom of the wise.

Perhaps it appeals to us at some very deep level of our souls because the story connects with our own essential, generic humanity, but without the enhancements of our culture, the pretenses of social rank and respectability, or illusions of righteousness. As we carry on our everyday lives wrapped in these socially generated constructions of meaning and security, we discover in the simplicity of the birth of the Savior that God meets us at a very different level of our being. God calls us back to ourselves and to the simple, fundamental necessities of our humanity soon to become apparent in the divine child himself: humility, honesty, fidelity, faith, and hope, love and reverence for the One who alone is holy. And like Mary, as we try to sort out the meaning of all that has happened, we must also take time to ponder what all of this will mean for us in the days to come.

What makes the story of Jesus' birth a timeless one is the fact that the people who followed Jesus did not follow him because they first knew of his divine, miraculous birth. It was only after they had been with him, listened to him, saw others healed by him or were healed themselves; only after they had experienced his suffering, his death and Resurrection did they come to understand the implications of their life brought on by the birth of Jesus. Leo the Great in confronting this same issue in the fifth century writes, "Invisible in his own nature he became visible in ours. Beyond our grasp, he chose to come within our grasp. Existing before time began, he began to exist at a moment in time. Incapable of suffering as God, he did not refuse to be a man, capable of suffering. Immortal, he chose to be subject to the laws of death."

Our familiarity with the story of Jesus' birth can also cause us to place a sentimental twist onto Luke's description of the event. It's a nice story that flows majestically , one that is not too much of a stretch to wrap our minds around. But the danger we needlessly create for ourselves is that we lose touch with its visceral charm that is so captivating to the soul. Before we are aware of it, its eternal truths have slipped through our fingers and we miss their implications, especially the ones that have to do with our well-being and that peace which surpasses all understanding.

But what speaks most clearly to us at Christmas as we gaze at the star of Bethlehem could very well be found in the somewhat despairing words penned generations before Christ. They are words, I suspect, that are not far from our hearts, captured by the psalmist. "*When I look at your heavens, the work of your fingers, the moon and the stars that you ha ve established; what are human beings that you are mindful of them, mortals that you care for them?*" (Psalm 8:3-4). As we reflect on these words the message could not be clearer. God is mindful of our human condition.

And so, we come to believe in Christmas---in Jesus as God incarnate---by experiencing the reality of Jesus as Lord of our lives. How there is no other who possesses his majesty and grace. How he lifts us and strengthens us and remakes like no other. How he humanizes us with his holiness be yond anything we could pull off on our own. How he releases us from the power of sin and the tyranny of death, and empowers us to become who God created us to be. It is in this the angels announcement, " *To you is born this day in the City if David a Savior, who is the Messiah, the Lord*" (Luke 2:11).

Who suspects that this baby born in the City of David will save us? That this baby born to Mary will bring us peace? That this baby's consistent, persistent, habitual, ordinary obedience to God will have an extraordinary, revolutionary impact? So let us now lay aside every weight, all our fr enetic, feverish bustling and acquiring, and adore the wonder of this love. Don't analyze, adore. Don't explain worship. Just be in the moment. Let Christmas act through you. Let the Word fill you with wordless grace and peace. In the words of the great hymn, "*Come, let us adore Him, Christ the Lord*" (Words by John Francis Wade, 1711-1786).

THE DOXOLOGY OF A NEW YEAR

Ephesians 1:3-6, 15-19a

The story is told of an Oxford professor who arrived at the train station too late for the train to London. Resigned to waiting in the station for the next train, he was surprised when the express train pulled in and stopped. So he opened the door, got aboard, and took a seat. The train started up and a few minutes later the conductor appeared. "Sir," the conductor said, this train doesn't stop here!" "I know, "replied the professor, "and I'm not in it."

I wonder if it isn't the same for us whenever we enter into a new calendar year. The year has arrived like an unexpected express train and we wonder whether we're in it or not. We, like Mary, ponder what the future has in store for us realizing the unknown has such a sense of mystery about it. As we approach the first Sunday of a brand new year, we assert a radical conviction: we are here for a purpose; we are alive for a reason. We affirm that the time we are given is not for crossing days off a calendar but for a much larger purpose, one that might not come to us naturally just as what came to Mary was not natural.

So the scripture begins where we are called to begin---with a doxology, a song of praise: "*Blessed be the God and Father of our Lord Jesus Christ, who has blessed us in Christ with every spiritual blessing in the heavenly places*" (Ephesians 1:3). The secular world does not begin the New Year with such doxological praise. For them God's wonderful gift to the world has been forgotten. The Church, on the other hand, stands over against the prevailing culture with the spirit of thankfulness in the afterglow of Christmas past. We mustn't forget that even though our lives have moved on from Bethlehem, God hasn't moved on from *us.* This story is about us, individuals who are part of God's family. It is humbling to think that the riches we enjoy as God's children were already flowing in our direction long before Bethlehem, right along with the light from ancient and distant stars that is just now reaching us. The apostle Paul gives us words of doxology to help us begin this New Year.

Just as we celebrate God's pride glowing over the manger, we are reminded it also glows over us where life's routine picks up once again. And as we walk through the months ahead there may be moments when we're not sure whether God loves us or whether we are included in God's beautiful promises. We may be so disappointed over our life or behavior that we feel no longer capable of being loved. But fortunately our faith is such that it is never static or complete. It continually changes, matures, becomes enriched and less self-centered as we lose ourselves more and more in the beauty and love of God reminding us in John-the-Baptist's words, *"God must increase; I must decrease."* The ultimate goal of all God's planning and work has nothing to do with whether we are successful or not. God is most concerned about our being filled with that which the culture is incapable of giving. It is what Paul so much wanted to give to the church in Ephesus.

The Ephesian Christians had grown to the point where their character and work had become widely known, and so, Paul gives thanks for that and in the same breath prays that it may get better. And he trusted that it would because behind and within the universe the very pulsating power of God was at work fulfilling his highest hopes for all of humankind. Paul begins his letter to the Ephesians in the same way he begins the others, *"Grace and peace from God our Father and the Lord Jesus Christ"* (1:2). It seems to be the way most early Christian letters began. Grace to you and peace, above all, says the apostle, because that is what God intended from the very beginning of everything. *"Before the creation of the world,"* God chose us in Christ to be *"holy and blameless in his sight"* (v.4) to be a blessing.

The cosmos, then, the whole creation is not some happenstance but rather an entity of God's own doing that moves purposefully in the direction of God's will to bless. The world becomes for us the theater where the drama of God's blessing takes place, which makes our life inevitably slanted to be a blessing to one another. It is the vocation we embrace as an outcome of our baptism. In Christ, Paul assures us, God has blessed us with every spiritual blessing as it has been from the very beginning. History flowing in the direction of grace and peace.

We see Paul's wisdom in crafting his greeting to the Ephesians in his use of words like "grace" and "peace" because for him they are what shape the future. Like Paul, there is much around us that causes us to wonder if grace and peace are anything more than words. We see war and hate and divisions. We hear bitter words; small, mean words; words hurting and distorting human life. Grace to you and peace, anyway, because everything that is not grace and peace cannot be from God.

Grace to you and peace because, of all the wonderful things we hope for one another in the year that awaits us, that is the best God gives us to give to each other. Grace to you and peace, we say to the world and to our neighbors. There is no point in a lovely church edifice except somehow to articulate God's will to bless. There are many who see the church as a business, and if that be the case, then grace and peace *is* our business, to speak God's blessing. But sometimes we need God's guidance to shape our lips around these kinds of words.

There are those occasions when the church must provide the words for people to say. At weddings, for example, when couples exchange vows with each other their lips must shape the words provided by the Prayer Book, ".....*To have and to hold from this day forward, for better for worse, for richer for poorer, in sickness and in health, to love and to cherish.....*" (*The Book of Common Prayer*, The Church Hymnal Corporation, New York, NY, p. 427). Those are not words we would have thought of on our own, or even words we necessarily want to use. We may even have found those words terribly painful; time and again we fail to live up to these brave words we pledge to one another, but when we strive to anchor a relationship in something more substantial than our own feelings, these are the kinds of words we seek to declare ourselves. We come to church to discover these words, especially, when we are called upon to offer something we do not have to give.

As we make our way into this brand new year, let us be mindful of the question first posed by thirteenth-century mystic, Meister Eckhart: "What good is it to me if Mary is full of grace and I am not also full of grace? What good is it to me for the creator to give birth to his Son if I do not also give birth to him in my time and my culture?" Let me put into context these words adapted from Psalm 19:14, "May the words of my mouth be shaped by grace, and may the meditation of our hearts be centered in peace, and may our trust be in You, O Lord our strength and our redeemer."

WRESTLING WITH OUR DISAPPOINTMENTS

Matthew 2:13-15, 19-23

For some strange reason the arrival of New Year's Day this time around is a much different feeling than the others. Life is not the same. It's a new era for all humanity in this generation and for those who follow. There is something in me that wants the world and myself to change for the better at Christmas, to become Utopia. I want all the problems of last year to stay put and not cross the boundary line into this fresh new year which has the potential of being one of real promise. I have this fantasy that wonderful, impossible things will happen in these days. The deadly sameness of life will be a thing of the past; the slate will be wiped clean; all the errors and sins and frustrations of the past will be left behind, never to be brought to mind again. And yet the cynical-self reminds me that this year is likely to be just a continuation of what'd gone on before.

This letdown after the spiritual and emotional high of Christmas is not unknown in the very story of Christmas itself as Matthew tells it. Following Jesus' birth Matthew records the visit of the Magi who, in the process, manage to foil Herod's attempt to locate the young Child. But realizing he had been tricked, Herod orders the massacre of all children under the age of two. Joseph is subsequently warned in a dream to escape with his family into Egypt lest he lose his newborn son to Herod's sword. So there it is, even in the New Testament, the joyful account of the birth of Jesus is placed back to back against the murder of innocents and exile of Joseph and Mary with the newborn Savior.

Whether we like it or not, as we enter the new year we must face the hard fact that we too are in exile. We are exiled from what is familiar and recognize that we are treading on soil that is in many ways foreign to us. We long for home and its familiarity and security. But while there are the Herod-types out there who serve no other purpose than to make life more uncertain and less secure for us, the power that Herod once wielded is now impotent, for the power now resides in the One who comes among us, our Savior, Jesus Christ. As the disappointments of last year advance forward unresolved and no less certain, we are gifted in the realization that Jesus' birth serves as a new beginning which can bring into balance those that continue to plague us. He prevents us from abandoning our faith over them. Phillips Brooks captured this when he wrote the words to his familiar hymn, "The hopes and fears of all the years are met in Thee tonight."

Every journey, every new year requires deliberate steps. We must take these before the pattern of balance becomes visible and the work of God is displayed. The first of these steps is a *Commitment of the heart*. As we sit in the comfort of our church early into the calendar year let us be clear that our commitment to God is first and foremost a matter of the heart. Augustine of Hippo knew well of the heart's restless until it dwells peacefully in God. So much of our problem-solving these days focuses on resolving them through our intellect. Having the answers is not as essential to living as is the sense of God's presence during dark season of questioning.

It was a famed Archbishop of Canterbury who reminded us that the longest journey in life is from the head to the heart. It is the heart in close communion with God that helps carry us through the pain, beyond the power of mere words. To whom does our heart belong? How will we know the answer to that question? It is what Solomon said, *"In all your ways acknowledge him."* It is the path we choose, the decisions we make, the way we live. If we do not acknowledge God, then our heart belongs to something or someone other than God.

While achieving balance amidst turbulent times is not dependent upon commitment of the intellect, in the second place, it does require *discipline of the mind*. When we have faith in God, it is less about making us more cerebral, and more about our faith affecting how we look at things. There was a famous American general during the Second World War who upon being informed by the enemy that his troops were completely surrounded on all sides said, "We have the opportunity to advance in any direction we choose!" A lesser general would have surrendered to the circumstances. If we do not believe that God is in control and has formed us for a purpose, we will flounder on the waters of purposelessness drowning in the currents and drifting further into nothingness.

The sixth chapter of Genesis describes every detail of the ark Noah was asked to build: how high, how wide, what kind of wood, the whole blueprint. Take your family. Everything is described for Noah except two vital details: there is neither a rudder nor a sail. Imagine preparing to be on water for forty days with nothing to control the direction of the ship! The very two items he needed to have at least some control are missing. Just when we think we've got everything in control, we'll discover we don't. Noah worked much harder listening to God and carrying out his instructions than trying to figure out how to keep his control on everything. It requires a disciplined mind to do this, one that more easily wraps itself around the ways of God than the ways of the world.

We must also be mindful of the significance of *recognizing of our ultimate purpose.* Joseph knew from his dream that being exiled in Egypt was not God's ultimate purpose for them, nor was Mary's pondering the angel Gabriel's message a sign that her hometown of Nazareth would be the last stop for her Son. But choosing to follow God's voice into exile was a piece of something much larger and purposeful. Faith is understanding that life has always been a process of being shaped and molded, of changing and becoming in such a way that---in the words of Jon Walton, "Of all the people that we might have been....and all the people that we aren't.....God has built on all the things that have been......to make us into the people that we are." Out of all that, our destiny is to be mindful that we are meant to be about the tasks that God directs us to, perhaps even taking us to places that we would not normally choose to go, coaxing out from us much that we do not believe we have. But to neglect answering the call would be to miss what our life is finally all about: discerning the life we were meant to live.

The angels may be gone from the heavens, the shepherds back in their fields, and the Holy Family away in Egypt. But the hope that was born at Christmas is not gone. Our moods have nothing to do with what God is doing on earth to usher in his Kingdom of peace and hope. Martyn Lloyd-Jones once preached a sermon in which he addressed the issues which we find familiar today. He said, "I do not care what the circumstances may be, the Christian should never be agitated.....at wit's end....never in a condition in which he feels lost......It implies a lack of trust and confidence in Him." Jesus was born in the days of Herod the king, a ruler of power and might. And from time to time his power is still seen. But what the world has not yet fully grasped is that these are now the days of Jesus Christ. And because of that, Herod's days are numbered. Take heart. The future is in God's hands, and so are we.

A CURIOUS GIFT

Matthew 2:1-12

The Magi traveled a long distance over the Arabian desert committed to following the bright star until it stopped, marking the spot where they would worship the Christ Child. Their first gesture upon arriving at the crèche was one of reverence, bowing down to show homage to the Child. Their visit culminated with the presentation of gifts of gold, frankincense, and myrrh. One can readily comprehend the purpose behind the giving of the gold and the frankincense to the Baby Jesus. Their utility is obvious. But the meaning behind the gift of myrrh is a bit puzzling when one considers its purpose.

In the ancient world, myrrh was a precious commodity, celebrated for its medicinal as well as aromatic properties. It was good for easing digestion, spreading warmth throughout a sick body, and as a disinfectant for clothes and bedding. Most famous of all, though, myrrh was celebrated for its use in embalming. A curious gift, it would seem, to take to the family of a newborn baby. A somber offering perhaps---one more suited to ease the ending of a life than to celebrate its beginning.

The Bible tells us quite explicitly that it was God's Word made flesh----fragile flesh to be sure; flesh subject to pain and weakening, and eventual death and anointing for burial--- descriptors that remind us that even at the beginning of Jesus' life Herod set out to kill the Holy Child. And a few years later, crowds from his own hometown attempted to throw him off a cliff. His closest friends denied him and fled from him at the perilous end. Throngs clamoring for his blood, crying "Crucify him!"

Myrrh is a bittersweet gift. Though we'd prefer to gloss over it, it reminds us that every birth is accompanied by a death of sorts. For if the true God is in fact the One who comes to dwell among us a Christmas and to be manifested to all the world at Epiphany, then all the other gods must perish. If we journey to Bethlehem with the Magi as adults with inquisitive minds and discerning hearts, we arrive with them at the manger of a death: the death of the gods we have created for ourselves out of our infatuation with success and popularity. We become radically cognizant that this is the death of our obsession with appearances; the death of our resigned insistence that we have everything all figured out, and that nothing---not even hope---can break into our world to surprise us anymore because we have seen the way life is and we are heart-sick, mind-sick and body-weary of it all. We come to the death of all our old, ego-encapsulated habits and are expected to bury them all under the straw behind the manger; and then to emerge into a strange new life---as if we, too, had somehow just been born.

In every birth there is an element of death. If we allow our minds to roam imaginatively around this text we will see the foreshadowing of the crucifixion weaving its way through the narrative. There's the thorny tree, whose resin glistens against the rough bark like drops of blood; the whiff of bittersweet fragrance, that remind us of how all that is precious in life is also passing. Perhaps then, we would be better off if we stopped trying to avoid such ominous shadows that clutter our lives; perhaps in these early days of the year while it's still fresh in our minds we need to surrender to our blind pursuit of unconditional happiness, and instead take a different road towards the abundantly more wholistic life of fulfillment by being faithful to God.

T.S. Eliot wrote a poem titled, "The Journey of the Magi," reflecting, many years later upon his pilgrimage place of holy birth. He writes of the harshness of travel, the regrets of leaving behind the comforts of home and the strange spiritual apparitions that point beyond themselves to the hidden workings of God's providence. With affecting understatement Eliot describes the encounter with the divine child in these words: "And arrived at evening, not a moment too soon. Finding the place it was (you may say) satisfactory." In other words, the end of his journey was a new beginning that opened up into new and great mysteries.

And while in every birth we are aware of an element of death, the Christian story handed down to us also proclaims that in every death there is the possibility of new birth. Out of the agony of crucifixion comes the amazement of resurrection. Out of the pain of separation in this world comes the joy of reunion in the life everlasting. Out of the ending of old habits of despair and resignation comes a new hope in the promises and providence of God.

Having made their visit to the Christ Child and given gifts, the Magi begin their long and arduous trek home. This time, however, they'll return a different way. As Matthew tells us, *"And having been warned in a dream not to return to Herod, they left for their own country by another road"* (v. 12). And while they altered their route to avoid going through Jerusalem again, it certainly wasn't the only thing about the Magi that had changed. Returning home by another route is a metaphor for living a changed life, and by their vulnerability in letting this holy moment speak to their hearts, the Magi could make a clean break with some past practices and habits and head home changed and chastened, molded to the shape of Christ's own triumph. This is how new life is created from the old.

In our lives we also may choose to "take another route" in light of our effectiveness as Christians in being "salt and light" to a fragile and broken world. We can decide to resist Herod in all his guises and go back home another way. We can resist all that childlike wonder, optimism, hope, imagination, play, creativity and adventure. We can also decide to pay close attention to all of life, including the silences, and to live less hurriedly and more openly and imaginatively so that we might catch sight of the glimmering star. Nearly everyone who encounters Jesus ends up going home another way. After they have met Jesus, they seem incapable---or certainly unwilling---to go back the same way they had come.

Fresh into this New Year our journey of faith can begin anew at the altar. And as we come forward to receive the bread and the wine---just as the Magi ate of the good news and drank in Christ's Incarnation---may our New Year's resolution reflect our willingness to go a new way into living our lives. May we be changed not just by the journey, but by our destination.

Epiphany

FINISHING WHAT GOD HAS BEGUN

Matthew 3:13-17

While we may not often think about it, when Christians gather for worship the one common denominator is their baptism, whether as infants or adults. Some will have no memory of their baptism, and others will be able to pull up from their memory every detail of their baptism. Regardless of which category we fall into, what's important is our discovering the meaning of it after the fact. It is often years later, as we make our way slowly into our journey of faith that the purpose begins to make sense. We discover what our baptism means after the event rather than before. The transformed community is the work of the church, ever expanding our capacity to transcend our individual approaches to life while engaging the work of Christ by way of his indwelling Spirit. Our lives are meant to be testimonies to the communities in which we live. Such transformation begins in the baptism of Jesus.

There is a bit of a hiccup in Matthew's gospel narrative as we note how Jesus' life skips from his infancy up to his life as a thirty-year old, leaving us rather clueless as to what happened in between. The text tells us that Jesus is eager to be baptized, and yet John hesitates. Jesus' baptism will help him learn who he is meant to be. Paul Tillich once commented on how Jesus is the only one who has been completely true to the voice he heard at his baptism, which went something like this, "You are my child. I love you. I am delighted with you." Jesus gave everything---his dreams and deeds, his labors and his life itself. So Jesus does not succumb to old age. He dies because he takes his baptism seriously. When Jesus cried out on the cross, "*It is finished,*" that marked the completion of his baptism.

Baptism, like most beginnings, finds meaning long after the event. The act of starting is itself often of little consequence. It's the finishing part that is difficult. When Bobby Knight was coaching basketball it has been said he would tell his players that it doesn't matter who starts. It's who finishes that matters. We must therefore ask ourselves if we have somehow come up short in our understanding of baptism when we see it primarily as giving access to "spiritual goods and services," rather than as a commission to be salt of the earth and light to the world.

Centuries earlier, in a similar manner, the first part of the prophet Isaiah's "Servant Songs" reminds us that in the Jewish tradition, being chosen by God came to be understood not so much as a privilege, but rather a challenge to be in service for the sake of the kingdom, "*Behold my servant, whom I uphold, my chosen, in whom my soul delights; I have put my Spirit upon him, he will bring forth justice to the nations*" (42:1). Traditionally, biblical scholars tell us, the servant to whom Isaiah refers was most likely pointing to the whole people of Israel rather than to a particular individual. Similarly, from the beginning of Christianity, followers of Jesus recognized his call to become a *people*, and just individuals, who poured out their lives in the service of others, in imitation of our Lord's own ministry.

And so, it makes sense that Jesus' baptism was not only an eloquent symbol of solidarity with those who heard John the Baptist's call to repentance, it also marked the beginning of his public life of service in God's vineyard. Nothing here is meant to deny the centrality of baptism, it being the means of a grace we receive as a divine gift. The emphasis here is the *effect* of that grace in our lives as Christians. While we may or may not recall our baptism, what's significant for us is that we understand and thus embody whatever meaning brought forth as a result of our living out the grace planted within us at the moment of our baptism.

In my role as a clergyman who prepares couples for marriage, I have discovered how easy it is for them to believe they are the perfect couple. On any given wedding day almost every couple is capable of creating a life together that brims with all the attributes of faith, hope, and love; and, as well, practically every couple is also capable of manufacturing something quite the opposite. The point being, marriage cannot be accurately judged on the wedding day. More often it is uncovered around the dinner table when the couple starts living in the real world. In the same way, neither can baptism be judged on the basis of what occurs on the day one is baptized. Beginning is usually easier than finishing. Someone once pointed out to me that every father looks good holding a newborn, but you cannot judge fathers in the maternity ward. Not until years later, when we look back on that child's life, will it be determined. Whether it's a wedding or a baptism, such celebrations find their ultimate meaning when we fulfill the promises that were made at the beginning.

I wonder how many of us, in the aftermath of the Christmas season, become aware of our insatiable appetite for new things. Asking ourselves "What's new?" is not a bad question, but if it reflects the character of one's own life day after day, then life becomes an endless parade of the next new thing. Perhaps it is best to be asking ourselves, "What's best?" I am betting on the fact that it is not the need for new things that we need as much as it is to understand the old beginnings. Is a new job, for instance, the fulfillment of a previous job? A new start may not be the thing that's needed to jump-start one's life. Instead, it may simply be to fulfill what has already previously begun.

In my pilgrimages to the Holy Land it has been customary to make a point of visiting the Jordan River where Jesus was baptized. Archeologists claim no actual location, but one place pilgrims often visit seems to fit how we imagine it might look. It never fails that someone requests to be re-baptized there in the Jordan. Their reason is often related to a significant change in one's Christian walk, and therefore wish to celebrate the occasion by being baptized again. But is this what is really needed here? A phrase from the Nicene Creed come to mind, "I believe in one baptism for the remission of sins." The best answer appears to be to finish what one has started; there is nothing wrong with the beginning. It's like handing someone a road map, someone once said, but then one has to take the trip.

The Roman god for the month of January was named Janus, from which we get the word "January." Janus was two-faced, looking in opposite directions. Janus describes very well our lives as we move forward into every calendar year, fully aware of the two faces we are capable of presenting to the world. Choosing to put on the face of the baptized, the decisions we make will be determined by how far we have come since we began the journey into baptism. Like it or not, our baptism has placed us squarely at odds with the prevailing culture in which we must struggle to figure out what's right and what's not.

Being baptized means that we tell the truth in a world that doesn't. We give in a world that takes. We love in a world that lusts. We serve in a world that wants nothing better than to be served. Whether we remember our baptism or not, its meaning is seen most clearly in the face we choose which will profoundly determine what we think, what we feel, and what exactly we will do today so that we may finish what God has begun in us. As Verna Dozier reminds us, "What happens on Sunday is not half as important as what happens Monday morning."

MEETING US WHEN IT MATTERS

John 2:1-11

As many of us have discovered, weddings can be challenging not only for the couple getting married, but for all who have a role in the ceremony. The larger the size of the wedding the more opportunity there is for glitches to occur. Fortunately, though, these often go unnoticed. But rather than a church setting, let us suppose the festivities are carried out over a span of several days, and often include a whole village. That is how it was back in Jesus' time. As John tells it, when the supply of wine is suddenly depleted in the middle of the wedding festivities the ramifications go viral in a matter of minutes.

The Wedding Feast at Cana marks one of the few appearances of Jesus' mother. In many ways she is the protagonist of this narrative, the catalyst for her son's first miracle. When it becomes evident the wine is gone, Mary looks to her son to handle the crisis at hand. Her insistence evokes a rather terse response from Jesus, *"Woman, what concern is that to you and to me?"* whereupon Jesus miraculously changes ordinary water into the finest of wines.

While this is Jesus' first miracle, John's story is not meant to impress us primarily as one of divine power, or to establish his credentials as a wonder-worker. If that were the case, certainly he could have picked a more lavish miracle than this. Nor is it necessarily a story about Jesus coming to the rescue. Rather, it is a story about life and abundance, God's unlimited, free flowing grace. Just when the wedding party is getting ready to return to the hard facts of daily life in a world of fierce competition for scarce resources, a new, hidden source of life and promise is revealed, and Jesus is right there among them. Rather than razzle-dazzle us, John is asking that we feel our way into the narrative, to savor its symbols. He wants us to begin thinking about what it is like to experience new life breaking into the old, familiar, ordinary circumstances of our lives, where the wine gives out too soon, times of celebration don't last long enough, and we are always worrying about whether there'll be enough.

A few years ago an Israeli airliner left the Tel Aviv airport bound for London. On board were generally two categories of passengers: there were Jewish people returning home after spending the Passover holiday in Jerusalem; and there were Christian people on their way home after celebrating Easter in the Holy Land. No doubt for many of them, it had been a pilgrimage, a holy journey to satisfy the spiritual longing to return to the origins of their faith. Many would inevitably report to friends back home their deeply moving religious experience. But was it really? What do they have to show for it? The answer is not likely to be found in the thousands of color pictures they took, or in the souvenirs that filled their luggage, nor in the memories of edifying and, perhaps, inspiring experiences. It resided in what it had done to them.

At one point during their flight to London it became known to the 450 passengers that one of them was someone other than a tourist. She was a four-year old Israeli girl whose liver had malfunctioned, and whose life was in jeopardy. Doctors in her native land told her parents that her only hope of survival was to undergo a liver transplant in England. They took her aboard that flight with no idea how they would pay for such an expensive operation. As the word about the little girl began to circulate among the passengers, an amazing thing happened. Someone began to pass the hat, and by the time all the passengers had put their gifts into it the hat, more than $73,000 had been raised.

When I came upon that story I had several immediate reactions: first, having been on several such pilgrimages myself, I was astonished that those people, at the end of their vacation, would have so much money left. It's not uncommon in these circumstances to either spend it all or over-spend. And further, it was nothing less than unbelievable that such an amount could have been raised in a matter of minutes, with no telethons, no pledge campaigns, no committee meetings, not even the offer of a tax deduction.

But the most important realization I made regarding that heartwarming incident was that those people aboard that plane had just been through a glorious, emotionally-laden religious experience in which they had felt close to God, and to the Risen Christ. Why shouldn't their hearts have been touchable, their consciences tender to the cry of a little girl whom they had never met? It is a gospel truth that when our God becomes known to us, God turns our attention not upon ourselves, but upon others who need us. At some point in our Christian walk with Christ, let's face it, our faith needs to "show up!"

Having witnessed first-hand Jesus' transformation of water into wine must have stretched how Mary envisioned her son's identity far beyond the boundaries of her understanding. Discovering Jesus to be other, and always more than we thought him to be surprisingly painful. John Henry Newman once observed how experiencing God's work within the world is, for humans, "like waiting and listening for a clock to strike, and yet when it does, it startles us."

Sometimes the church has forgotten that our Lord once attended a wedding feast and said yes to gladness and joy. We have forgotten how Jesus provided a peculiar lesson of encouragement and comfort, turning the weaker into the stronger, the common into the precious, the tasteless into that which gladdens the heart, a sampling of how Christ deals with the souls of those who place themselves into his hands. The Season of Epiphany is a good time to remind ourselves that wherever Christ is made manifest, the best is saved for the last. Jesus came, as he says later, that we might have life in all its fullness (10:10). Sometimes the church has forgotten to live the joy of such exorbitant generosity and to toast the world with the incredible good news of grace.

Much of what we encounter in life is dependent upon whether we stop at the identification of good wine or seek beyond the wine the divine manifestation it represents. When Christ draws us into fellowship with him, much like he did to those around him at the wedding feast, he shares with us the costly vision of human hurt and need that fills our world. Christ also shares a commitment, like the one he made at Cana---and again at Gethsemane---of letting our will be ruled by God's agenda of the Kingdom of heaven on earth, become our own. Transformation only came when someone took Mary's words seriously, *"Do whatever he tells you."* Jesus teaching the Word of God isn't about knowing stuff; it's about doing stuff.

DISCIPLESHIP AT FAITH LEVEL

Matthew 4:12-23

Nineteenth century Danish philosopher Soren Kierkegaard did not mince words when writing about the Church and its stewardship of what he often referred to as "the divine call to faith." His take on faith was that it could not, should not present itself falsely as something that fits neatly and reverently into our well-ordered lives. Our text from Matthew offers us an example of Jesus breaking into the lives of four men with a proposal which, as they soon find out, does not necessarily fit neatly into their well-ordered lives. Jesus beckons and, without questioning, four fishermen lay aside their tools of the trade and follow.

Not all of us are blessed with such simple assurance. Perhaps we are more like Paul on the road to Damascus or Moses at the burning bush. We would just as soon turn deaf ears to God's summons. But these fishermen have seen Jesus before; they have spoken to him. He is the one John the Baptist introduced them to earlier. They were the most unlikely leaders; not one of them was a priest, rabbi, elder, or prophet. None are connected in any way to the life of the Temple. As the Bible tells it, most knew more about mending nets than winning converts when Jesus said he would make them "fishers of men." Jesus stands on the lakeshore in broad daylight and asks Peter, Andrew, and James and John to follow, and assures them that if they do, their job descriptions will change and so will their lives. While their lives may not have been technically without God up to this point, theirs has been a life that has yet to cultivate the kind of adoring dependency that is required to experience Jesus most fully and to be most powerfully used by him.

They made their living by feeding people from the realm of the unseen, the waters of the Sea of Galilee. Jesus watched as they set out from the shore in hope and determination of finding a "treasure" hidden amidst the waves. They were searching for what was not apparent, but nevertheless present before them. But now they turn inland and fish for people. No boat, no nets, no apparent expertise among them all. Jesus does not ask them to believe anything in particular. They need not adhere to any dogma or display any kind of aptitude for this vocation. Trust is the real issue here. Jesus did not leave recruitment up to someone else. He, and he alone, wanted to be the one to teach them that what was unseen can be made manifest in order to feed that which is seen. The personal encounter with Christ is the central element to participation *in* and the formation *of* Christian community. In the words of Dietrich Bonhoeffer, who experienced personally life in community, "We have one another only through Christ; but through Christ we do have one another, wholly, and for all eternity."

While the use of imagery does help in capturing our attention, there is a downside to pushing the "fishing for people" too far. For instance, in our modern everyday world we don't necessarily hook and land unsuspecting members. Neither do we cast our nets in order to haul in the next Bible class. It is doubtful Jesus had anything like this in mind when he called out to Peter and Andrew along the Galilean shoreline. Jesus, a carpenter by trade, begins a conversation with fishermen, and yet he speaks *their* language and is on *their* turf. Fishing is their vocation and they know a lot about it, and this is precisely where Jesus begins. He starts with what *they* know rather than what *he* knows. In our case Jesus begins not with what *he* knows, but what *we* know. It begins not with what *he* does best, but what *we* do best. Jesus assures us that we can do it because it is not so different from what we have already done. Jesus Christ always begins right where we are.

This of course is where our identity, not just individually as Christians, but as the Church begins its own formation and where our destiny finds its roots. When Jesus calls us to be the Church, it's not just any church he has in mind. We are not called to be the church of "what happened then," or "what's happening now." We are called to be the church of "what's happening next," more than contemporary, more than traditional. God's is a transformational enterprise, moving the real and actual to what it *can* become, what it *will* become. Unlike the well-intended plans and strategies we set for ourselves, God's clear plan is for us to be able to look back two-thousand years and discover that all over the world there are apostles still drawing people in.

I often wonder what it was like back then for them to be called by Jesus. Although the Gospels suggest that Peter and Andrew unhesitatingly left their work to follow the Lord, their decision must have been deeply heart-felt and difficult to make. Note that neither of them threw out the option of staying busy in their pursuit of fish in Galilee while somehow fitting Jesus into their lives as needed. Interestingly, I have found busyness for God has not drawn me closer to God. In fact, in some ways it creates a false, and perhaps even dangerous, sense of spirituality. It causes one to assume that spirituality is a performance; that intimacy with God is a business arrangement. The result is a spirituality devoid of meaning, hope, and, most importantly, intimacy with God. I came upon what for me represents a glimpse into what Jesus' call to ministry must have felt like, as expressed in the popular hymn by John L. Bell to the traditional Scottish hymn, Kelvingrove. Its first stanza asks, "*Will you come and follow me if I but call your name? Will you go where you don't know and never be the same? Will you let my love be shown, will you let my name be known? Will you let my life be grown in you and you in me?*" ("The Summons" in *Gather Comprehensive*, Chicago: CIA Publications, 1994), 700.

This hymn quite pointedly is direct in its questions as it relates to our willingness to serve, which is what Jesus' call in the Matthew text is essentially about. It's a two-fold summons that is both personal and radically challenging. Harkening back to the God of Abraham, Jesus invites the disciples by name to step into a country they do not know and be transformed forever. It is a summons not unlike that of master to disciple, not merely a call to learn about a particular way of life, but to *become* a way of life. It is an invitation, after all, to never be the same again.

Notice also how Jesus' summons draws us to each other so that at its core our lives and our livelihood center on bringing to light the importance of our relationships with others. Catching fish may be an honest way to earn a living. But we eat in order to live in community with others, and what we do should be focused on that instead of the other way around. It guides us as we make our way forward to the place where everyone's job can be a vocation and where we yearn to understand the ways of God so that we may embody the disposition to love God.

In a dialogue sermon preached several years ago by Catherine Gonzalez and Don Wardlaw on *The Protestant Hour,* they succinctly describe the role of faith in responding to a call: "Faith somehow means to be open to guidance; be willing to leave that which must be left; being willing to stay and reorder that which must be reordered, but at the same time to be open; so that when we are called, who we really is a response to God and not the pressures we feel around us" (Atlanta: PRTVC), Jan. 26, 1975. Jesus doesn't move relationships along too quickly. We can all measure the time frame it took for us to drop our nets and follow. Perhaps there are some yet to make that decision. We know that a call from Jesus is authentic when a change of mind leads to a change of conduct, which leads to a change of character, which ultimately leads to a change in destiny. Now take a deep breath...and follow.

A MOMENT OF INARTICULATE AWE

Luke 2:22-40

A peasant couple takes their newly born child to the Temple to offer a sacrifice to the Lord as their Jewish faith requires. And then, led by the Spirit of God, an old man approaches them and, taking the child in his arms, and with an abiding sense of awe, begins to sing a song of salvation. It is one whose words have been echoing inside his head for years, and the same ones I remember singing every Sunday as a young lad in the Men and Boys Choir of the church our family attended, *"Lord, now lettest thou thy servant depart in peace, according to thy word; for mine eyes have seen thy salvation,"* (vs. 29-30 KJV). Paul Woodruff captures such a moment in his book, *Reverence: Renewing a Forgotten Virtue*, "Reverence is an ancient virtue that survives among us in half-forgotten patterns of civility, in moments of inarticulate awe." The feeling Simeon must have felt is comparable to a slave receiving freedom. It sounds as though Simeon was quoting the prophet Isaiah directly. Generations before, Isaiah had been so sure that when God's light finally came it would be for all people---not just for Israel, but for the Gentiles---and now Simeon was announcing the same thing. The child in his arm, he believes, is like a lens through which the old man sees all of life. Jesus is what the past was leading to, making the present worth living. Jesus controls the future, and now, satisfied that all is and will be well, Simeon asks to die, but not before testifying to what he has seen and heard.

Such a response would not be unlike that of those who would come to follow Jesus later in his adult life. It is a teaching moment, a modern-day reminder of how, like Simeon, the original disciples came to testify to what they had seen and heard, and yet, how we, as disciples under similar circumstances, are more inclined to rely on what we have read and rationalized. There are simply some events that bring our entire lives into focus. Jesus is sufficient for us to see God and discover who we should be. And while Simeon doesn't perceive every fact and facet, he knows it is enough for him to discern the outline of a life that comes together like two sides folded in the middle. He sees. He understands. He praises God in song because he has learned to see God at work in the ordinary. Subsequently, it is by the stuff and bother of everyday living that God's voice is heard and the warmth of God's presence intimately felt. It is through the broken muffler, the mislaid bill now overdue, and the checkbook mistake, that the Word comes like music to the ears. It comes to us so softly we cannot hear it because of it being muted by the noise of the living. Luke's Gospel records that, "*inspired by the Spirit,* [*Simeon*] *came into the temple*" (v. 27 RSV). Notice how Simeon was not looking "in the church," for the Savior, rather he was outside the temple at first "on the street." Where are we looking for the face of the Savior today? Do we look with expectation upon the crowd gathered outside the church, examining every face for the Christ within? Are we poised like Simeon caught up in doing acts of kindness and justice? If we are, the face of Salvation is still among the nameless crowd which moves silently past our churches in every city. Are we poised sufficiently enough to find them?

I wonder what else Simeon saw, this old man with a gift for discerning the meaning hidden in the heart of the everyday. Perhaps the only way we can fully open our eyes and see God's gift is, taking a lesson from Simeon, by engaging regularly in the disciplined life of prayer, fasting, and worship. Only then can we be readily available and willing to recognize God's greatest gift through the eyes of Simeon, whose life was both in sync with the Temple and coupled with a piousness molded by the God venerated within its walls. His faith drew its inspiration from the environment which daily enveloped him.

It was typical for Simeon in his role as a temple priest that on the Sabbath witnessing the crowds lined up outside the temple, he would stand erect at the entrance and with a loud voice call out the psalm. The gathered assembly, in unison, would sing a question asking permission to come and worship. The priest's response would include a description of those permitted to enter.

After all, the approach to the precincts of the sacred required integrity of conduct for all who entered through its portals. To dwell with God, as their tradition had instructed them, required that they must dwell rightly and act righteously on a daily basis in the ordinary business of their interaction with friends, neighbors, and the poor and vulnerable, as a basis for entering in to worship. For us church-going people we tend to err on the side that believes the only quality for worship is merely to show up. The Hebrew faith, on the other hand, was more stringent in requiring that the way one lived outside the walls of the sanctuary had everything to do with whether one could truly worship inside the sanctuary. Simeon's soul was like a sacred vessel which, as a devout man of God, nourished his deep and abiding sense of expectation, not unlike that which was proclaimed by the prophet Isaiah centuries before. A genuine sense of worship integrated within an abiding and sincere faith in God's promise of salvation are what brought Simeon to the place where he could recognize the nearness of God's presence. His priestly vocation in the environs of temple life served to transform him, animating his every move and thought towards the God who promised that one day the light of Salvation would come and enter into his longing soul and bring delight to his heart.

We moderns hesitate to admit it, but truth be known, we still struggle with this very issue, often looking for worship that fits comfortably into our lives rather than worship that actually changes our lives to fit the truth which confronts us in worship. The faith of a Simeon recognizes that worship reflects as much as it shapes who we are. We don't pray in church in order to catch up on our praying as if pursuing some sort of quota. We pray each Sunday so that when Monday rolls around, and before we get out of bed or as we drive to work, when we see something wonderful or when our hearts break, we'll be moved to pray. After all, we don't give an offering when the plate is passed so that we don't have to give anymore. We give to become generous people. We don't see friends on Sunday so that we can forget them the rest of the week. We come to remember that God calls us to live as a family with those who join us in worshiping our Lord and with those who never will. In the same way poets are

word-struck and romantics are love-struck, people who worship---
like Simeon and the prophetess Anna---are God struck.

The text from Luke's Gospel is yet another Epiphany story---
referred to as The Presentation---another instance in which Jesus
is recognized for who he is, and his work described as having a
particular mission not only for the Jews, *"The glory to thy people
Israel,"* but to us as well, *"a light for the revelation to the Gentiles"*
(v. 32 RSV). Even as reported earlier in Matthew's Gospel, the
three Magi saw in this no ordinary child and by their homage
acknowledged him as king beyond the tiny realm of his birth, so
too with Simeon who sees the same thing in the same child. And
he claims for Jesus not just his family and not just the people, but
the entire world for all time, including you and me, we who have
not seen and were not there, but who are in some measure cast in
the beam of that light, this "light to enlighten the Gentiles." A
baby is born; he is named, and an old man sings. And nothing is
the same ever again.

HOPE IS FOR TODAY

Luke 4:16-30

Jesus has returned home, has spoken with authority about his identity, and now the hometown folks are amazed. They are abuzz with platitudes, *"Is this not Joseph's son?"* (v.22). Flush with the revelation of Jesus' identity they stake their claim; "He's our boy!" The crowd feels they are among the privileged to receive an inordinate amount of blessings, especially when it comes from one of their own. At first blush it appears they are trying to somehow control the identity of Jesus by putting him in a box, the box of special privilege, which would ensure them of their cherished place and a personal dose of Jesus' power.

The crowd, however, is totally unaware that since those earlier years Jesus has met John the Baptist at the river Jordan. What's more, he not only heard John preach, but was baptized by him and had sensed the touch of the very Spirit of God. And so, when Jesus returned to his hometown it was not as a carpenter's son, but as both a teacher and preacher. On this particular day he was asked to read the appointed text from Isaiah's prophecy, an inspiring testament to the Jews, who by now had grown weary of the heavy-handed rule of Imperial Rome. It forecast a new day when fortunes would be reversed and God's people would be free. When Jesus finished, he rolled up the scroll and announced that today, this text which you have just heard, has come true. Professor Fred Craddock has often pointed out that, according to Luke, the first recorded word of Jesus' public ministry is "today." Today this text has come true. The kingdom is present today. God's promises are fulfilled today. Not tomorrow. Not someday. The word to the Nazareth congregation, and undoubtedly to the Church, is, "today." But as you can imagine what Jesus announced did not set well with the constituency gathered before him, so much so that they attempt to toss Jesus over a nearby cliff. Unfortunate for them, they did not see what Jesus saw, a roadmap laid out before them, and each of them prominently placed at the center.

I find it truly amazing how God is manifest in and through the work of Jesus, sometimes in surprising, disturbing, or even infuriating ways. It appears the crowd in Nazareth, while appearing outwardly pious, has allowed the cultural norms embedded in their culture to have more and more of the upper hand in terms of shaping their identity and determining which values they will embrace, while at the same time discounting the prophets. Jesus was not going to play it safe, in Nazareth or anywhere else. "What it means," Jesus is telling them, "is that the Messiah, God's deliverer, has been sent not to set you free from your Roman captors, nor to bring you wealth, not even to lower your taxes, but to present God to the outsider because you won't do it." Their preference for building a better synagogue than a better community becomes obvious. It is easier to envision their own future off in the distance, rather than God's, today.

In his book, *Subversive Spirituality*, Eugene Peterson writes, "For God is not an object that I deal with, but a subject who speaks to and addresses me" (p. 27). People speak and people listen. We can be emotionally struck by the aesthetics of a particular object. But it is our interaction with another person---what we see and hear---that allows the message to flow through us. In order to become tea, water must first flow through the tea leaves. That is the only way for transformation to occur. Jesus' audience must allow his words to flow through them, to permeate their soul, for them to establish any meaningful dialogue with Jesus and, subsequently, animate the entirety of their being.

There is a powerful connection between the announcement of the coming day of God and its emergence into being fully real and tangible. Part of the tremendous answer to the riddle of Jesus' comment, "*Today this scripture has been fulfilled*," is its fulfillment as the words are spoken and heard. But since they haven't flowed through those on the receiving end, they are unable to see what Jesus sees. The fulfillment of scripture referred to by Jesus is a new renaissance changing the way the people of God think about God and the world, about what God is up to in the world and what part they play in it. Living into the vision makes it visible. As an old fairytale reminds us, frogs must be kissed while yet frogs, before they are seen for what they really are, princes or anything else.

Imagine if you will, what if we began to hear our Scripture, not just as a historical record of what God did in some bygone era, but as the living story that shapes us and identifies those of us who are unwilling to limit our spiritual lives to so called "church involvement," preferring to build our lives around our convictions and taking to the streets with abandon. In the words of Heraclitus, "Whoever cannot seek the unforeseen sees nothing, for the known way is an impasse." Those hearing Jesus made every attempt to protect themselves by making Jesus something he was not rather than bless and serve outsiders. They seemed unable to see the distinction between belonging to the synagogue, and *being* the synagogue. The issue for us is not necessarily about *belonging* to a particular church, it is about *being* the church. The first generation of Christians would likely not have been familiar with a phrase such as, "going to church" (or what was then their place of worship) for the simple reason that their concept of church was as a verb rather than a noun, their faith in Christ was very much tied to their very being rather than merely something they did. A further illustration might be to imagine two fish swimming in a fish bowl and one fish says, "Let's go swimming." That wouldn't make any sense at all since swimming was the essence of their being fish. We don't "do" church, we *are* the church.

When Jesus unfurls the scroll from Isaiah and announces that he is the embodiment of, as Isaiah has described, the "Servant of the Lord," he discloses the *why* of the Incarnation. In Jesus, God sets out to deliver humanity from that which it cannot extricate itself---the grip of evil. "*Deliver us from evil,*" we recite each Sunday from The Lord's Prayer. The crowd, upon hearing Jesus, thought to themselves in words something like, "This God is dangerous!" And yet I wonder, when was the last time---and under what circumstances---a church got into an uproar over God's grace being "too gracious, too unlimited, or too boundless?" Frankly, God's style of love is a challenge for all of us who follow Jesus, and a threat to the world's power structures, precisely because it is ecstatic, overflowing its own boundaries and, moreover, keeps nothing for itself.

Whenever we read the newspaper we often discover that the first page is filled with crime, scandal, and violence of all sorts. Articles about scout troops, church picnics, Golden Wedding anniversaries, and academic achievements appear further back, often buried among a myriad of colorful advertisements. If there had been a newspaper in Bethlehem on Christmas Day when Jesus Christ was born, page one would have covered news about such characters as Emperor Caesar Augustus, Quirinius of Syria, and Herod, quisling king of Judea. Somewhere on page five there might have been a mention of the "strange happenings" that surrounded the birth of a baby in a stall behind an inn. Ever since the birth of Christ, the "page five" news of the Incarnation has been decisively shaping human history. The hope for the Church and its mission is to be decisive enough to believe that "page five" news is what determines "page one," which, providentially, is the prologue to our future. May we hunger for journalists who can tell us what God is up to *today*.

THE CHALLENGE OF MAKING CHOICES

Deuteronomy 30:15-20

During their long journey through the wilderness, the Israelites had several times turned away from the Lord, but then the time would come when they would inevitably return to their God. Theirs was a constant struggle, despite the harshness of desert life, to remain steadfast in faith to the One who had brought them this far in their journey out of bondage towards the land God had promised them. For them each day was life and death and the possibility to choose between the two. The text from Deuteronomy could not be more fundamental. Moses throws down the gauntlet as he demands that they choose between God and their former ways. The life Moses urges the Israelites to choose is anything but tidy. In fact, it is the very thing their parents stumbled over, the life they had denied, the life the first generation of the Exodus passed up forty years earlier when they were faced with a choice along the banks of the Jordan River. Whereas they had failed to love and obey enough to get across the river and into the Promised Land, now, the second generation, is being given the opportunity to make a giant leap of faith. Moses exhorts the grandchildren of the Exodus to find their spiritual nerve.

Can we---broken and sinful in our mortal flesh---really choose life? Saint Augustine and his reforming heirs in the western church believed that passages such as this one are generally understood as revelations of our inability to choose life; we can only lament our alienation from life. And yet our Christian tradition recognizes our dependence upon God to bring us life and fellowship with our Lord. So in addition to contemplating our ability (or inability) to be righteous, this passage points toward the God who desires us to abide in the life God has graciously provided us. In addition to sharing the divine prerogative of choice, God also promises to be with us each day as we contemplate choices that tend either toward life or death. After all, God is not simply a promise for a distant future, but the present intimacy of God.

As we have all experienced, life is full of choices. Many of them we easily spot, such as what to eat for breakfast or what we will wear today. But there are many others that come along we do not recognize. Most of the potential choices in life pass by unnoticed, in part because of the habits we have formed, for good or ill. We follow our usual ways of doing and thinking without ever being aware of it. Habits serve us well if they are life affirming and up to date. On the other hand, habits can also be destructive to us and those around us, the demands don't mesh with the times. While they have a way of resisting change, every now and then, something or someone jars us out of our habits, confronting us head-on with our complacency and opening up our eyes to see something marvelously new. We must re-examine our habits, asking whether or not they are serving us well. It is only when we take our lives off auto-pilot and begin to seriously take control of the steering wheel again that we can truly choose what is best for us.

But of course, there are times when the issue is not so much about being unaware of our choices as it is about being painfully aware that our choices are limited. We want to have a choice, but are convinced we have no choice. We may feel trapped and not have the choices we would enjoy having and subsequently are faced with choosing between "honorable mentions" on either side of the issue. But there is the option of choosing not to choose. We can choose to do nothing. Often people with very few choices, like a patient who is dying, feel empowered when they suddenly become aware that, in fact, they are choosing. If all else falls flat, as Victor Frankl reminded us years ago, we can choose the attitude we wish to have in an otherwise helpless situation. In other words, by claiming our choices, however limited and few they might be, empowers us, gives us the semblance of control and sense of dignity. Life, in good course, becomes very interesting when our choices are as clear as they appear to be in Deuteronomy.

What are the implications of "Life" in the imperative "Choose Life?" Those two words go hand-in-hand. It is sobering how often we choose, consciously or unconsciously, to engage in non-life affirming activities, to take one step away from life towards death. For example, we know we have moved away from life when we speak of attending church as opposed to worshipping God. Moses as a prophet found he had to remind the Israelites, whose view had been nothing but wilderness, that life is not without meaning. In modern parlance, it is not about the pursuit of money or longing for a good retirement. Life is about God. Moses stood with the children of Israel at the edge of the Promised Land and challenged them to choose life. We might think that when we are given the choice of blessings or curses, joy or ingratitude, we would always be drawn towards life. But there us something in every one of us that is afraid of life and drawn to mediocrity. Writer Calvin Trillin writes, "I've always thought that it must be sadder to be a businessman without money than, say, a poet without money or a coal miner without money. You've failed at the very game you signed up to play" (*About Alice*, N.Y., Random House, 2006, 22).

There is a connection in the text that brings this story forward to us. Just as Moses led his people out of captivity and bondage in Egypt through the waters of the Red Sea, likewise, the second generation must cross through the waters of the Jordan River. Roughly twelve-hundred later, Jesus would be baptized in these same waters at the hands of John the Baptist. This would become for all who would follow Jesus a ritual cleansing, an outward act as a means to confirm a new beginning for us, and along with it a promise to choose life over death. God wants us to be a caring, courageous and strong people. God wants us to be among the people who make the church holy. God wants us to live sacred lives. God wants us to have the stamina to choose life. As Anne Lamott writes in *Grace Eventually*, "God is waiting for us to notice that life is good. God is waiting to enter our lives like a track coach for slow people" (p.11). Yes, the Season of Epiphany and its many manifestations of Christ is a good time to remind ourselves that life is good.

Naturally, we don't choose everything that happens to us. But the God we worship can guide us in our decisions to opt for life and the hope of the Spirit in a multitude of ways. Professor Brett Younger, McAfee School of Theology, recommends "holding our cheerful friends especially close. Pointing things out to people we love and paying attention when they point out things to us. Learning things we have told ourselves we would never learn. Playing with children as Jesus did; laughing often, long and loud; being patient with our own imperfections as well as the imperfections of others; surrounding ourselves with what we love; paying attention to the deepest joys, the joy of the church acting like church, of neighbors becoming real neighbors, young people finding their life's purpose" (*Lectionary Homiletic,* Vol. XXII, No. 2, p. 21). This is powerful stuff!

We face a decision at our own Jordan River in the same way our ancestors did. Discernment is best engaged when we pray for God to change us in ways we haven't begun to imagine. Perhaps choosing to live a genuinely holy life, one we can be proud of; opening our hearts to the Spirit; search for something deeper and better than our own comfort. With such foundational issues addressed we can then choose to let God make our lives wonderful.

GETTING FAITH IN FOCUS

Matthew 17:1-9

There are many of us, I am reasonably certain, who have had a "mountaintop" experience. Sometimes we are surprised when they occur and other times we are in awe of the experience. We often recall such moments years later as if it occurred yesterday. But I wonder if we remember what was going on in our lives when we encountered such moments. The mountain moments in the Scriptures often come in the midst of human dysfunction and confusion. We recall from the Old Testament that before Moses climbs the mountain, the Israelites, whom he had previously led through the Red Sea to freedom, appear to be confused and lost. Their days of enslavement in Egypt have slipped from their memory and, unfortunately, so has their vision of the Promised Land. They have become bitter and now are bickering against Moses. When Moses finally makes his way down the mountain he finds them worshiping the golden calf---promiscuous believer concerned only with whatever feels good. It is only the mountain moments in between that keep Moses going, reminding him of God's faithfulness and giving him the vision, the energy, and hope to get through the muck of human imperfection he finds himself immersed in.

Things are not that much different as Matthew records. Peter, James, and John become awestruck when confronted by God on the Mount of the Transfiguration. They are terrified and confused when the One they have been following is suddenly and without warning transfigured in a bright and glistening aura of light right before their eyes. But, funny thing, they are also changed. Unable to take their wide-eyed gaze off Jesus, the three disciples are overcome by a transforming holiness from which they inherit a fresh openness to mystery. Why wouldn't anyone want to take advantage of an opportunity to actually listen to their soul, leave business-as-usual, climb up the mountain, stick their head into the clouds, and open wide to the presence of God?

Mark Twain once remarked, "You can't depend on your eyes when your imagination is out of focus." Have you experienced times when the immanence and transcendence of God have come together, when the clouds have opened up and the boundary between the universe and you has vanished? Have you experienced moments of eternity you wish you could bottle and keep forever? While we may not always be aware of it, God does give us such moments. But, unfortunately, not everyone recognizes them for what they are. Fourteenth century mystic and theologian Meister Eckhart writes, "God does not work in all hearts alike but according to the preparation and sensitivity he finds in each." To our own detriment we have gotten used to placing ourselves at the center of the world and judging everything we experience on the basis of our own limited and imperfect methods.

The Transfiguration of Christ on the top of a mountain isn't something the disciples are ever able to explain. This remarkable phenomena is not something they are able to make something out of. Rather, it is something from outside which makes something out of them. As Matthew tells the story, immediately following the spectacle of brilliant light Peter puts forward what he anticipates will be a helpful suggestion: *"Lord, it is good for us to be here; if you wish, I will make three dwellings here, one for you, one for Moses, and one for Elijah"* (v. 4). Peter tries so hard, but nowhere does the disciple's handbook address what to do in case of transfiguration. Peter has a hard time sitting still and wants so much to do something. Perhaps his response is not far from how we would respond under similar conditions. At issue here is our responsiveness to God breaking into our lives, especially when it is neither expected nor, in some instances, wanted.

When we speak of transcendence we're referencing a God beyond both our imagination and our experience, whether it's an imagination in or out of focus. God is bigger than our ability to comprehend, smaller than we scrutinize, wider than we dare extend our realm of belief. And when the unimaginable becomes unglued before our eyes, and God suddenly comes into view, we are faced with the unenviable task of pondering how to respond when God no longer fits our God-sized spaces? How do we wrap our human logic around something for which we have no precedent? Fortunately, though, God comes to meet us in such times when we are pushed beyond ourselves. But if we lose touch with such moments, if we turn our backs on them and neglect to stop occasionally to notice what is unfolding around and outside us, we run the risk of missing God and losing ourselves at the same time.

If Peter were to learn anything from his experience on the mountain it would be, like it or not, transfiguration changes everything. It forces us to look in the mirror and ask what God is doing in our lives because that's what it will take if we are to stop constructing dwellings shaped by outdated blue prints, old rules, and the old precedents. Only then do we allow ourselves to detach from familiar surroundings and structures, and finally release our grip on disordered attachments as we are opened to God's presence. In his book of prayers, United Methodist Bishop Ted Loder writes, "O Timeless God for whom I do not have time, catch me with a sudden stab of beauty or pain or regret that will catch me for a moment and make me look hard at myself---the unutterable terror and hope within me---and, so, to be caught by you."

Rather than trying to make his experience atop the mountain permanent, it would have been much better had Peter heeded God's declaration and drew himself towards Jesus and, with an audience of one, listen to his voice. This is how God addresses the limitations we place on our clouded thinking and vision, pointing us in the direction of Jesus by saying, "*Listen to him*" (v. 5c). Jesuit priest Walter Burghardt reminds us that "Listen" spoken from the clouds invites us to a multi-dimensional exercise of listening. Firstly is the invitation to listen to one another, for to do so is to risk and be vulnerable with others, an act of love in itself. We should also, he says, listen to Jesus, and hear the word of the living God both in scripture and then in our hearts. But finally we should listen to the world around us, for it allows us, as Burghardt writes, "to hear God speaking in the majesty of creation, through history, and through our interacting with others" (*Sir, We would Like to See Jesus*, Paulist Press, 1982, 41.)

The story of the Transfiguration, from which the church proceeds into Lent, begs the question each of us must address: what are we truly seeking? The answer depends on what we see and hear and experience, as well as how we interpret the extraordinary and discern its meaning for our life thereafter. I find it amazing how providentially we find ourselves on the top of our own mountains. No matter how much we try, we cannot plan or stage such moments in our lives. One mountain moment is all we need for us to be changed forever, reborn in the image of God. As Jesus makes his way down the mountain of Transfiguration he stares straight ahead. Listen to him, "There is one more mountain to climb, in Jerusalem."

Lent

A COVENANT IN SPITE OF US

Genesis 9:8-17

At the time Isaac Newton graduated from Cambridge University in 1665, people believed that white light was the purest form of light, and thus that colored light was somehow impure. To test this belief, Newton shone a beam of sunlight into a spectrum of colors which he concluded are also seen in rainbows and are the fundamental colors seen by the human eye.

In the ninth chapter of Genesis is a story of deliverance and new beginnings as evidenced by the presence of a rainbow. It is the conclusion of the story of Noah and the Great Flood. Called into being out of chaos and nothingness at creation by the breath of God, humanity seems at every turn bent on returning to chaos and nothingness, and so God floods the earth. Because it is in God's nature to save and create, and rather than destroy all things, God determines instead to wipe the slate clean and start again. Never again will God destroy the earth in such a way, and as a symbol of this covenant a rainbow appears. It is shaped like an archer's bow, but it is an undrawn bow. From a Christian perspective, the trajectory of the undrawn bow extends through the prophets all the way to the cross. Later in the biblical narrative we discover that the God who grieves for a flooded creation experiences deeper suffering in the passion and death of Jesus.

The story of the flood and the rainbow are singularly fitting to ponder at the beginning of Lent. It tells us about ourselves, but it also tells us about God and the lengths to which God is willing to go for us and our salvation. Wickedness, or at least one stage of it, had perished in the Flood. But God was starting over with the family of Noah and was preserving the diversity of life symbolized by the many colors present in the rainbow. Despite God's awareness that the evil inclination continued to be an element of human nature, God resolved to find another way of dealing with it.

What guarantee is there that if God starts over again things won't end up hopeless? The flood is not imposed by a remote tyrant, but a God who actually grieves for the destruction of creation. This a God who recognizes that after the flood human inclinations remain unchanged, and perhaps have even gotten worse than before. In the aftermath God pledges a dependable natural order that never again will be universally destroyed by floodwaters. The text of the new agreement reveals that nothing whatsoever is required of creation. It sets limits only upon God, a God who chooses to abandon strict retribution, who resolves to re-claim the world in spite of human sin.

We are all guilty of falling back on the notion that God gives us what we deserve as a reason to give others what they deserve. But in actuality God does not give us what we deserve. God loves us and sticks with us and chides us and encourages us even though we are undeserving. God's warm sun continues to shine upon us, and God's gentle rain continues to fall upon us, no matter how unjust and evil we may be. According to the apostle Paul, "*It was while we were yet sinners that Christ died for us*" (Romans 5:8). If that is the way God acts towards us, shouldn't we also act that way towards others? As such, we are called to carefully examine our relationships with each other, and, indeed, our connection with all of creation.

It must have been tremendously comforting for Noah to hear words of hope coming from God, especially having been tossed about aimlessly on that enormous body of dark water. When navigating through the uncertainties of life, we, too, can appreciate that same sense of hope and trust that we are not left utterly alone. How reassuring it must have been for Noah to hear about God's intentions. I am reminded of God's words to Israel in Jeremiah's day, "'*For surely I know the plans I have for you,' says* the Lord, 'plans for your welfare and not for harm, to give you a future with hope'" (Jer. 29:11). God wanted Noah to believe that God's desire for him and his family was a future with hope, but at the same time, not devoid of suffering.

I remember several years ago sitting with a young man whose background of abuse and neglect served to shape his world. He was sitting in a jail cell the morning after a tragic late-night quarrel with his wife. In the midst of the melee in which a gun had been introduced, she was shot and killed. It was a few hours later in the morning when I showed up at the jail. He sat alone in a cramped and pungent cell, accused of a crime the details of which were still a blur. His struggle to surrender his life over to Christ was palpable because he couldn't get past the issue of how Christ could possibly love him and wished him no harm. He was convinced God hated him and desired nothing for him but endless suffering. I gave him a Bible to read, the pages of which he immediately began to devour. It was not until he came to the part where he discovered how God's plan of redemption was as true for him as it was for anybody else that his life began to move for the first time in the direction of healing and health and, yes, even resurrection.

The charges against him were eventually reduced and after serving his one-year sentence, was released.   When by happenstance I encountered him several years later, I didn't recognize him. He was by this time clean shaven, dressed in a suit and told me he had accepted Christ into his heart and gotten married to a lovely young lady.   Together with his spouse he was serving as a counselor at a treatment center for addicted teenagers. Despite the tragic circumstances of a troubled life, God had given him a new beginning and a clean slate.

God's being *for* us does not preclude suffering and pain. After God's covenant with Noah, things did not go especially well. As Mark records in his gospel, after Jesus was baptized in the Jordan with the word of Jesus' belovedness accompanied by the symbol of a dove, Jesus is immediately driven into the wilderness where he was tempted, not once, but three times. God's faithfulness to us does not excuse us from having difficult times in life. God keeps the future open by self-limitation when we threaten to close off hope by unlimited repeat offenses. God's will for us is good. As Paula D'Arcy often shares in her retreats, "God comes to us disguised as our life."

A mother and her daughter were taking a walk following a rain shower when they spotted a beautiful rainbow. Gazing up in amazement the little girl asked, "Can we take that with us and put it in our house?" Imagine for a moment what would have happened. A house transformed, containing the glory of the rainbow and its many colors. What does the Body of Christ look like in the light of the rainbow? Taken seriously and intentionally, it would profoundly change a faith community. Not into something perfect, but a place where people were willing to let their hearts be remade in the image of God's heart; a place where people would let their hearts be open, with grief over their hardened hearts and that of the world's. The patience and forgiveness spilling forth from hearts broken open by God's love may paint the walls of the church, color its people, and emanate from its doors and windows into the world. We simply need to ask with wonder, "Can we take the rainbow home and put it in our house?"

LEARNING TO DANCE WITH GOD

Genesis 15:1-12, 17-18

In his characterization of religion G.K. Chesterton wrote, "Let your religion be less a theory and more a love affair." Abram had been aware of God's claim on his life for a long time. It is as if God decided to deal, not with the whole earth and all at once, but with an individual people and a bit at a time. The spotlight is on Abram. The wanderer will have a home, a land later called Israel. It will be willed with his offspring, a mighty nation. Finally, by or through these people, all other nations of the world will receive the blessings of God. Abram is like a funnel through whom God pours a blessing that will cover, as was intended, the whole earth. It begins with an introduction and a promise; it ends with acceptance. Shall we dance?

This is what God always had in mind. It is trust that stands in sharp contrast to shame and guilt (as in the garden), to anger and fear (as with Cain), to ceaseless activity (as with the Tower of Babel). Entering into the covenant is entering into the dance. This movement is now called "righteousness." The "reward" is the dance itself. We can either stand here, each in our own little world, frightened and afraid of what the future holds, or we can create a future together.

There are times in life when we, like Abram, have misgivings about the future. The guidance we received as we stepped out in faith and trust no longer seems true, and the way ahead no longer clear. How is it possible for God's blessing to come upon Abram and Sara and their seed if there was no child, no heir of God's promise? Abram had already been promised a new land under his leadership and blessings for him and his wife and generations to follow. Why the questions, the hesitation? Why shy away from the dance? Perhaps it is this incredible generosity that is so difficult for many to accept. Is it just too good to be true?

The Bible is full of instances which reveal the generosity of God. God comes to us ready to bless; our impatience doesn't change God. God comes to us hoping we will be trusting. We do not need to understand God's blessings fully in order to enjoy them. The God whom we see in this story from Genesis is a promising God, a God whose love is bound by a pledge that must be made good through time over a dangerous and uncertain path of history. It is a strong, promissory love to be redeemed by faithfulness through time. H. Richard Neibuhr steadfastly maintained that the first response of humanity toward God is that we don't trust God. I wonder if it isn't the promise itself that is giving us the problem.

How are we to understand a promise? Someone once described a promise as a word given now that binds its maker to actions performed and relationships maintained in the future. This makes a promise rather risky. Its original motives may fade. The context and circumstances may change to the point where the promise must sometimes be either re-thought or abandoned altogether, or perhaps simply maintained as is. Yet at its core, the promise is the supreme expression of love. A love that promises is a love that seeks to endure beyond the ebb and flow of history. It transcends the effects of time. Promissory love, the heart of the covenant made to Abram, is loved that reaches for Eternity. Yet, as is well known, the history of promising is largely a history of failure, frustration, and broken trust. It is the response of faith and the cry of doubt, the trusting heart and the questioning soul that provoke Abram's approach to God's generosity.

Inherent in God's gracious generosity, though, there is something of a warning. If we, like Abram, and like his distant spiritual successor Job, venture to question God and demand proofs of God's good purposes, we are warned here to be prepared for answers that are, frankly, unsettling. For to him, who demanded to know, was revealed the terrible knowledge of suffering yet to come. To wrestle with God for answers, as Jacob learned with his angel in the night, is to come to a knowledge that wounds. Jacob came from his ordeal with a displaced hip joint. To know the God of Abram, Job, and Jacob in the intimacy and anguish of God' covenantal encounter is to be wounded. It is to enter into the unfathomable mystery of God's transcending purpose which is forever seeking by way of the cross to bring resurrection, faithfulness, and life to light through the darkness of our sin and suffering.

Abram recalls God's consolation when God tells him not to be afraid because God is his shield; your reward will be great. But Abram nevertheless still brings his questions to God with a reminder that he is still childless, things aren't happening. Then he tells God what he plans to do about it---since God doesn't appear to be doing anything. We tend to take matters into our own hands when God doesn't come through according to our timetable and expectations. Abram brings his own ideas to God and then listens. "Count the stars," God tells Abram. This is the sign, which is a clue to God's movement seen in everyday reality. *"So shall your descendants be."* Gradually the questions and fear which had come to haunt and harass Abram lose their grip on his mind and soul. Peace descends gently into his heart. The text says Abram *"believed the Lord"* (v. 6). But how does that play out in our lives?

Abram believes but still asks questions. Immediately after God called Abram's faith righteous, Abram is reminded that the one who brought him from Ur of the Chaldeans and gave him the land is none other than God. But Abram wants to know how he can be sure of that. This is not necessarily a lack of faith on Abram's part, but is a sign of his questioning faithfulness, a pleading with God for more information, more clarity, more courage, and more commitment, striving to follow the steps God calls us to on our own journey of faith. God comes to us ready to bless.

How tempting it is to construct a future of our own over which we have a modicum of control. Take the lead in the dance; the partner is too cumbersome. Better yet, cut lose and go solo. To trust God's future is a radical action because everything changes, we discover for ourselves who we really are in the eyes of God. Abram is now a believer, he holds on tight and waits for the cue; he rests in the arms of the promise giver. The faith of Abram and the faithfulness of God are thematic partners in the biblical ballet. Can Abram trust God? Is his God a God who can be trusted? Frederick Buechner reminds us, "Faith is the direction your feet start to move when you find that you are loved." Shall we dance?

A GOD WITH PLANS

Exodus 3:1-14

A popular children's hymn reminds us "This is holy ground, we're standing on holy ground, for the Lord is present and where he is holy..." As the text from Exodus tells us, Moses takes off his sandals to approach the burning bush, not because he first recognizes it as holy ground, but because God tells him to. Trying to live as godly people isn't easy, as Moses' story reminds us. Fleeing from killing an Egyptian taskmaster, Moses winds up in Midian where he takes on a wife and subsequently becomes an employee of his father-in-law. One day at sunset Moses notices something out of the corner of his eye bright and shining like a bush on fire. It is here that the destiny of history meets the journey of one man. It is God in the bush, and a voice says to Moses, *"I have seen the misery of my people. I have heard their anguish, and I know their sufferings"* (v. 7). God calls Moses to go back to Egypt and lead the nation of Hebrews out from under the yoke of Pharaoh and on to their promised land. Moses objects at first, but then finally agrees to trust God and go where God is sending him.

In a posting from is blog, Brother David Vryhof SSJE writes that "when God commands, we should listen, because God is not only asking something from us but is also offering to do something for us" (Society of St. John the Evangelist, Cambridge, MA). Without Moses being aware of it, throughout his life God was progressively shaping Moses, and now it would take on its final shape as Moses becomes the means by which God's will is accomplished on earth. This is a story of a God with plans which intersect with our plans and who sets us to doing what we would not otherwise plan on doing. God works in us so unexpectedly. Though we can't say precisely who God is, we can celebrate what God does.

All of us get caught up in whatever life throws our way, so much so that we don't even notice that all about us are plans not of our own making and forces that shape us over which we have no control. But then God enters our orbit and we are surprised to realize that our lives are intended to be lived and used in ways we had not seen. Have we ever noticed the movement of forces in our lives that have made us what and who we are, that have placed us in this moment and have made us the right person to be doing what God intends for our sake and for the sake of others? Likewise, any number of things could have prevented such an encounter with Moses and the burning bush. What would have happened had Moses not been curious? How often is one's attention drawn to a burning bush in the barren countryside? Suppose he had been sleeping, nodding off like the disciples in the Garden of Gethsemane. What if he had never fled from Egypt? We can all come up with reasons why this encounter might not have occurred.

But the point is not the "what ifs" of our lives. The point is our understanding that life in general has always been a process of changing and becoming. Much having occurred without our knowing, but nevertheless in such a way that of all the people that we might have been, and all the people we aren't, God has built on all things that have been to make us into the people that we have become. We are meant to discern and to fulfill our calling, to be about the tasks God has chosen for us to be engaged in doing. We must never forget that by not answering the call God has placed before us would be to miss what life is finally all about: the life we are meant to live.

Could it be that the life we've been given is unfolding exactly the way it was meant to unfold. That God, whose eye is on the sparrow and who numbers every hair on our head, has put it into our hearts the truth that we must follow, the work we must do, the calling that is uniquely ours, the direction we must go. Like a burning bush within us, all that has gone before in our lives is leading us to all that will now be.

The great prophet and leader, the one who goes to the top of the mountain to get the Ten Commandments directly from God, is the Moses we all remember. But it is important for us also to remember the Moses who is wandering around in the wilderness, performing the menial job of looking after his father-in-law's animals. The Moses who has no great career aspirations, no obvious traits for leadership, no apparent deep spirituality or faith. This Moses may have more to teach us than the Moses on the mountaintop consulting face-to-face with God. This Moses shows us that it is in the ordinary experiences of our everyday routines that we are most likely to encounter the divine, there in the all-too-familiar landscape, out of the corner of our eye. That is where we meet God and find our destiny. It is there that we learn God's name, and in a sense learn the meaning of our own. Frederick Buechner reminds us, "Nobody had ever known God's name before Moses did, and nobody would ever have known it afterwards except for his having passed it on; and with that thought in his heart up on Pisgah, and with that name on his lips, and with the sunset in his whiskers, [Moses] became in the end a kind of burning bush himself" (*Peculiar Treasures*, Harper & Row, 1979, p. 112).

Perhaps that is our destiny, too, to be a kind of burning bush ourselves, the fire on our faces and the blaze in our hearts as we live the life God has called us to live, knowing that not to do so would be to not live at all. In the case of Moses, he acts initially as if an encounter with God is the last thing on his mind. Seeing a bush aglow with fire and yet not consumed is just a visual curiosity for Moses. Only when he hears God's voice does he understand this curiosity to be an appearance of God.

Through this Moses became aware of some aspects about his relationship to God that were disconcerting. The first concern he had was about the voice of God that came to him from the burning bush and how it was probably not the God Moses wanted. But then, who goes out with a fire in their belly to lead a nation because of the God they would rather have. No homemade deity could lead a people through the trials they would soon face over the next forty years. Moses also discovered that being called by God can also mean that what God desires *from* us is the same as what God desires *for* us. In Moses' case God was not only asking something from him but was also offering to do something for him: The courage to confront Pharaoh and the stamina to lead

God's people. Finally, it became apparent to Moses that God is not demystified through further understanding. In fact, the more one understands God, the more mysterious God becomes. The more you know, the more you don't know you know. We are summoned, each of us, to go to that place in our lives that is burning like a bush. Look carefully for you will be standing on holy ground.

FLOWING WATER TO RECKON WITH

John 4:5-42

Second century bishop, Irenaeus, says, "The Church is the fountain of the living water that flows to us from the heart of Christ. Where the Church is, there is the Spirit of God, and where the Spirit of God is, there is the Church and all grace." The Church, filled with God's Spirit, he reminds us, is not just the recipient of this grace, but becomes the steward of all grace. This grace flowing outwards to others has been entrusted by God to us (*"Adversus Haereses"*). We control the spigot.

A woman comes to draw water from the well, where she encounters a stranger. This man, a Jew whose people were at daggers drawn about their traditional religion, takes her beyond the surface realities of her life to uncover a deeper thirst, deeper than the water she has come to draw. Her life is forever changed. In all likelihood she was not the president of the local Junior League or anything like that. Let's just say whoever she was, she was not the pillar of the community. Even though nowhere in the story is it mentioned that this Samaritan woman was a "sinner," we catch a glimpse of what she's been up to when Jesus divulges her marital history and her current living arrangement. The well is at the center of a town that serves as a crossroads of two well-travelled highways, an excellent location for one who, as we say, "gets around."

Rabbi Edwin Friedman often emphasized in his writings the importance of not only being self-differentiated but also having the skills to maintain one's boundaries, especially when entering into emotionally unhealthy environments or, as he often referred to them, "anxious systems." The benefit, as we discover, allows us to stay connected to others without being absorbed into their troubled environment. It is this protective barrier that allows us to maintain our healthy status regardless of whatever is going on around us. But this line of thinking also works the other way, especially when we create fences or walls that keep us intentionally isolated from the so called "undesirables." This could have been a regular occurrence among those who visited the well. But not for Jesus.

Probing our own lives is likely to expose instances when we have placed boundaries around us for all the wrong reasons. In his work on *Soul Making* Alan Jones reminds us that everything that happens to Christ happens to us. The author is not suggesting that the same things literally happen at the same time, in the same fashion as they did for Jesus. But our lives as Christians follow a cycle similar in nature to what our Lord experienced. We have a birth, a growing up, our own "wilderness" temptation, times of discerning vocation, times of spiritual ecstasy, times of suffering for and with others, and, of course, a time to die and to be raised up in Resurrection light.

In his own obedience to God, Jesus does the unimaginable. Facing ridicule and social "contamination" in daring to speak publicly to an unknown woman, standing to lose whatever privilege and prestige he has earned (as if he wanted it in the first place), Jesus nevertheless speaks to her. In doing so, his "ethnic pride" as a Jew has to be swallowed. The conceptual categories of "chosen people" versus "rejected people" have to be reexamined. Likewise, *what happens to Jesus happens to us.* One way or another, we will inevitably be asked to break our most "sacred" boundaries, our most "cherished" beliefs for God's sake---and ultimately for our own.

The Gospel will not leave us the same because with God as the third partner in our encounter with others we are left free to be human, no longer needing boundaries to protect us from "the undesirables." The chance encounter at Jacob's well embodies a grace filled life in which God's Spirit brings into our lives a new way of responding to others, a "nonconformist" response, like a "new wine" poured into us that calls for a response that the old wineskins simply can no longer hold. Boundaries and rules will be defied---traditions trampled---not merely to make us a different people, but instead, servants obedient to Christ and instruments of his grace.

In the introduction to Jo hn Sanford's classic work, *The Kingdom Within* (HarperCollins Publishers, New York, NY), he shares a personal vignette from his early youth. Coming out of the Depression, his family decided to modernize their house, adding electricity and plumbing. A deep artesian well was drilled to replace the old one which was sealed over. Years later, attempting to get fresh water from the old well he discovered it was bone dry. It seems that wells of this size are fed by hundreds of tiny rivulets along which seep a steady flow of water. Interestingly, as water is drawn from the well, more water moves along the rivulets, keeping these tiny apertures open. The dryness of the well was not because there was no water, but because it had not been used. Our love can be much like that, sometimes flowing abundantly outward towards others, and other times not at all. Love can dry up and the soul become barren if the living water of God doesn't flow into us---and into the gathered community. When out of neglect we become dry, God is not dead. We are. The remedy to quenching this thirst is a long drink of the Holy Spirit to start the stream flowing again. Remember, this woman at the well not only felt Jesus' unconditional love, she went back to her village astonished at Jesus' sincerity, " *He told me everything I ever did"* (v. 29). John's Gospel tells us many Samaritans came to believe in Jesus because of what this woman said. Yes, this fallen, rejected woman becomes the first evangelist in the gospel of John---the first one to tell with passionate joy, the Good News of the Gospel. He is the God who sees us as we are. He is the God who empowers us to become who we still need to be. God works supernaturally in very natural ways.

When we first laid eyes on her she was a shadow of what God created her to be. She had been used and abused by people in the town and wanted nothing to do with anyone who took advantage of her. That's the reason she came to the well during the hottest part of the day when everyone else was cooling off in the shade. Little did she know that the vi sit to the well would bring her God's offer of a new kind of life for all who give up the stagnant water and come to him for the livi ng variety. Could there not be such a reflection flowing in us and from us that others---known or unknown to us---might be drawn to come and see who relationship Jesus really is, and discover for themselves what an authentic relationship[with Jesus looks like for them? Jeanne Francois de Chantal writes, "Hell is full of the talented, but Heaven of the energetic."

SURELY WE ARE NOT BLIND

John 9:1-41

Noted playwright George Bernard Shaw once observed that "All great truths begin as blasphemies." Such is the case according to John's Gospel as Jesus reminds his audience how he is the light of the world. The irony is that the seemingly "holy" Pharisees---the virtuous, the intellectual, the well-respected---refuse to see the power of this light at work right before their very own eyes, while this previously blind beggar who, as the Pharisees claim, has been "born entirely in sins," never waivers in his belief. It is a story about a blind man whom Jesus causes to see; it is also a story of the spiritual blindness among those who are offended by this sign of Jesus. Imagine someone saying, "Just because *you* had a holy moment with mud doesn't mean that the rest of *us* will stop scraping it off our shoes!"

As the story goes, Jesus recognizes an opening for "God's works to be revealed," while the disciples see a way to lay blame. Jesus see in this an opportunity to transform evil; the disciples find a way to talk about it. Jesus views the man from the future; the disciples view him in terms of the past. Jesus sees redemption; the disciples see guilt. The question that confronts us---indeed, convicts us---is whether we see people as problems to be solved (or reflected on), or as people in need of God's love and our care. After the blind man is healed---a healing which, by the way, never mentions his faith in Jesus---the only one who appears to be able to rejoice in the cure is the man himself. All the Pharisees can manage is to be outrageously offended.

While pondering the restoration of sight to a man who has yet to see the light of day, in the aftermath the deeper issue is quite simply that of being nearsighted. Such an anomaly is common to persons of all faiths who have made tradition, dogma, or duty more important than God. They are convinced God's actions towards them must coincide with their understanding and fit within their own prejudices, otherwise they simply aren't valid.

We fall victim when proximate truth morphs into ultimate truth; there is no possibility for God to go beyond the boundaries of our own understanding. It is God in the box, but it's my box, a springboard from which to launch our doubts concerning God's working in someone else's life. One person's ecstatic moment with mud usually looks, to the rest of us, like a classic case of self-delusion.

C.S. Lewis made an observation in a speech to the Oxford Socratic Society that was related to our becoming better participants in the mission of God. He professed to the gathering, "I believe in Christianity as I believe that the sun has risen; not only because I see it, but because by it I see everything else." And so, the pathway to being able to "see everything else" through the lens of our faith begins when we possess enough gumption to point out our own spiritual blind spots.

The most important truth easily lost to our spiritual blindness is, remarkably, the Lordship of Christ and his coming to heal and to save. He *is* the Light of the World. When the disciples try to press him to explain why bad things happen to people and why he is able to put things right, Jesus makes it clear that it is his authority that shows forth. We recognize that Jesus is in charge of the "why" question, as the Scriptures remind us, "*he was born blind so that God's works might be revealed in him*" (v. 3). It is not the role of the disciples to understand the mind of God. There are times when, in attempting to bring comfort to others, we fall prey to the same temptation as the disciples. We assume it is our job to provide convenient answers to "why," but end up making matters worse for the person we are trying to help.

The blind man has no intention of staying in the "why," instead he eagerly moves to the "what now?" In the past, everyone was eager to learn why he was *blind*. And now they want to know why he was *healed*. All he can respond with is simply, "*He put clay on my eyes, and I washed, and I see*" (v. 11). It is hard to miss the nuance coming from the newly-healed man in terms of how he *confesses* Jesus rather than *explain* Jesus. Instead of this being an occasion for the gathered assembly to celebrate and be reconciled to each other, the religious leaders scornfully refuse to admit their own shortcomings and toss the man out of the synagogue.

If there is anything about our faith that is hard to grasp it is when impossible things happen to improbable people. It seems to prick our innate discomfort with mystery and block what we are capable of seeing but somehow don't. Struggling to provide reasons for another's illness, we avoid having to admit the degree of mystery that envelopes human suffering. It is tragic that the Pharisees miss seeing altogether the man's healing as an act of God's grace. To them the issue becomes a theological problem, something to be debated.

Interestingly, Jesus is absent from much of John's narrative. It is the man whose sight has been restored who comes to center stage. He is the one facing the barrage of questions from the Pharisees, and as he proceeds to answer what he knows to be true and moves closer to the truth about Jesus, his interrogators resist it more and more. Unlike them, the man gives no evidence of being bothered with all the verbia ge coming his way and, at the same time, has no hesitation in te lling them what he doesn't know. But the one thing he does know for sure is that "once he was blind and now he can see." As he is forced to reiterate this irrefutable truth, the veil is lifted as to the identity of this man who has given him his sight; first he is just a man called Jesus, then he is a prophet, then he is "from God," and finally he is "Lord." Eyes wide open, he sees in every sense of the word.

The Pharisees provide us an example of how we protect ourselves against new truth by asserting the old truth. If we say something loud enough and often enough, maybe it will conquer the emerging truth that feels very much like a threat to us. In his book, *Christ on Trial*, Rowan Williams says that "when God's truth comes to light, it puts us on tria l. God's truth in Jesus unsettles our judgment in devastating ways, causing us to question everything we thought we knew about how the world's supposed to work" (Wm. B. Eerdmans Publishing Co., 2003). Note how almost everybody fails the man born blind. The community fails. The religious authorities fail. The family fails. The only trustworthy figures in this stor y are the man who is healed and the man who healed him, Jesus. The light of the world shines bright and everybody else shuts their eyes in self-defense because that's the natural thing to do. But this story is not about what comes natural. It is about what doesn't come natural. We don't need to shut our eyes; we will not be blinded by the light. We will be saved.

It is no wonder early Christian historians have reported that this story was etched on the walls of many catacombs of the first century. Down in the lightless recesses of these tombs, strangely, these Christians could still see. They claimed the waters of baptism had washed away a blindness that no darkness could overcome. Perhaps Lent is a good time to give serious thought to etching this on the walls of the lightless recesses of our own tombs so that we, too, can see what we are missing.

STARING DOWN THE SERPENT

Numbers 21:4-9

If one wishes to venture into the deep regions of the soul in Lent, such a journey (real or imagined) must include time spent in the desert of our own introspection and barrenness. The Book of Numbers recalls the years when the Israelites wandered in the wilderness following their Exodus from Egypt. Instead of being a glorious trek to the land of promise in Canaan it became instead a period of discontent characterized by complaints over the leadership of Moses and Aaron, and a rebellion against God. The synopsis of the reading centers on Moses who is experiencing nothing but heartache from the Israelites who describe captivity in Egypt as if it were Camelot. As if hunger and thirst were not enough, suddenly are set upon by serpents that bite and sting. Moses' subsequent prayer to God is answered with a command to replicate a bronze serpent and place it on a pole as protection against the deadly poison. Those bitten are instructed to look upwards at the bronze serpent and thus live, the serpent symbolizing God's mercy and healing power, which they are free to reject.

This story, this strange, striking, scary, unsettling tale is about decisions and their consequences. Someone once observed that in addressing questions of eternity, it becomes easier to understand why there are theologians who are uncomfortable with the eternal ramifications of our lives resting on the decisions we make. This perhaps could be the reason why some Christians find themselves pulled towards the concept of predestination---the idea that eternal destiny is unrelated to human choice. Big decisions, they maintain, shouldn't be left to human beings. Instead, they should be left to God. Brett Younger of McAfee School of Theology goes so far as to suggest that Universalism, the belief that God accepts everyone into eternity unchanged, is attractive because it places much less significance on our decisions. Our minds, he says, convince us that all paths end up converging. In other words, it doesn't matter what anyone thinks or what they decide because everything will turn out the same in the end.

Israel was bitten by the serpent of fear insofar as they did not place their future in God's hands. Like those wilderness wanderers, God has given us the wonderful, at times painful, gift of choice, a product of our free will. We have to decide to look up and see the life God offers. We choose in the words we speak, the words we don't speak, the people we love, the people we don't even see, the thoughts we entertain, the ideas we hold, the deeds we do, and the deeds we leave undone. We choose death or life. Just as the pole with the bronze serpent symbolized healing and life to the ancient Israelites, the cross symbolizes eternal life to those who make the decision to follow Jesus.

The author of John's Gospel remembers this story and records that it is almost like that bronze snake when Christ is lifted up so that all can see the passionate love of God. The cross itself is strange, scary, and unsettling. Christ's death reveals the extent of God's mercy for all of those who are snake-bitten by the lingering power of death. It is not the cross that heals so much as it is the expression of love behind the cross. These two strange stories, the snake and the cross, are both about God's grace.

The fact that God does not chase snakes away, but instead offers the people a way of hope in the midst of them, is God's way of placing responsibility on the people for their own well-being, just as they must also claim responsibility for the consequences of their whining and murmuring. God saves the Israelites, but not without their own response, for as the scripture remind us, they must be near enough to the bronze snake to see it and must look at it in order to live. The failure to trust God---and God's intermediary, Moses---is the basic issue. Moses didn't throw down the gauntlet for the people to believe in some doctrine of God. Moses was being diligent in trying to nudge the people forward trusting that God would honor the divine commitment to lead them to a new land. At the same time, God was placing the onus on them to take that thing which was the primary evidence of their sin and guilt and fear---to take the snake itself---and gaze straight at it. No longer were they to imagine it as a source of evil and destruction, but to understand how God has transformed the predicament and utilizes the serpent as a source of healing. That's where hope resides. But when people choose not to place their trust in God, it can be as deadly as a poisonous snakebite.

There are elements in every one of us that God would have us lift up into the sunlight of love and take a good, long look at. In *Mere Christianity*, C.S. Lewis writes that "every time you make a choice you are turning the central part of you that chooses, into something a little different from what it was before. Taking your life as a whole, with all your innumerable choices, all your life you are slowly turning this central thing....either into a creature that is in harmony with God, and with other creatures, and with itself, or else into one that is in a state of war and hatred with God, and with its fellow creatures, and with itself" (Harper Collins Edition, New York, NY., 2001, p. 92). Lewis is suggesting that from the first choice we make in the morning until we choose to go to sleep at night, we are making the decisions that form our lives as an expression of what God has granted us. When we don't have the courage to choose what's best, but act as if our choices don't matter, we're not likely to make much progress even on the smoothest path, but when we choose courageously we go forward even on the roughest road.

Even if we get rid of all the bizarre stuff---the manna, the poisonous serpents, and the snake on a stick---this story still sounds peculiar to modern ears for the obvious reason that the difference between life and death is one of those decisions. The text points out to us that the answer to the Israelites wandering in the wilderness is in their choosing to lift their eyes to see death on a pole. Shortly, the Church will once again remind us that the answer to our wandering in the wilderness of our sin is when the Son of Man is lifted high on the cross, the ultimate symbol of God's love for the world.

While we may struggle to fit our minds around this story and its implications for us, what is nevertheless obvious is that the path to redemption always takes us into our own wilderness for a time. Healing comes not from the serpents that would destroy us, but from God, from doing what God instructs us to do: choosing to stare down the serpents that have plagued us, and believe---perhaps for the first time---they can be transformed into a source of healing. And as we make our way out of our wilderness, let us trust that God's hand is present in all that unfolds before us, the things that at face value may not make much sense, such as, the cure for a snake is a snake. The cure for human life is one man's life. The cure for death is death. You know, there is a lot of healing in that---because it works.

A CLASH OF WORLDVIEWS

Luke 23:1-49

The kingdom of God is clashing with the kingdoms of Rome and the temple. Swords are drawn. Threats are made. The Messiah mocked. The cross kills. Meanwhile, Judas betrays, Peter denies, and women weep. But there is also another clash that unravels on Calvary---two condemned thieves hanging beside Jesus, one on the left and the other on the right, have last words with him. For all practical purposes they represent two clashing worldviews. Like the rest of Luke's narrative, the dialogue between Jesus and the two criminals makes God's mercy visible to us.

What Jesus hears coming from the two thieves could easily have come from our lips on any given day. We are not told what crimes were committed, but Jesus, like so much of his public ministry, spends his last moments with two marginalized members of society. One of them remains hard of heart with his words, *"Save yourself and us"* (v. 39). The other merely wants to be remembered when Jesus comes unto his kingdom. Their mindsets live side by side within us in a constant battle of wills.

In the first instance we see an unrepentant thief who is unable to trust, and till the very end refuses to surrender his "what's in it for me" attitude. In his world sin is all right, as long as you get away with it, or, still worse, hold to the belief that there is no such thing as sin at all. God, if God does indeed even exist, could care less what certain segments of corporate America do for profit, how many disenfranchised people we choose to ignore, or how many relationships we have a part in destroying. When the end approaches, such people are likely to demand of Jesus that not only should he save himself, but themselves, too.

Our culture has a word for that worldview. Estrangement. Paul Tillich has argued that estrangement is the basic human condition. His belief is that we are separated from our true and best selves. We are separated from God's best intention for us. The inevitable result is personal guilt and universal tragedy (*Systematic Theology*, Vol. I, Univ. of Chicago Press, 1951). The whole sad story of Jesus' last days---the way the crowds turned on him after Palm Sunday, the way he was abandoned by his closest friends, the condemnation by authorities, and, finally, the killing of Jesus---is not merely a story about crooks and evildoers. Instead, it is a story about the failure of people like us, people who are trying to do their best. In failing to recognize that hope rests in the grace of God rather than in one's own goodness, the unrepentant thief missed an opportune moment to give it up and come clean and radically alter the inevitable consequences he faced because of what he had done.

On the opposite side, the so-called "repentant" thief acknowledges that he is receiving the punishment his deeds deserve. He asks only that Jesus will remember him when he enters his kingdom. He confesses his sinfulness, makes no demand on Jesus, and, perhaps for the first time in his life, allows himself to hope and trust in this innocent man dying next to him. Jesus is moved by what he hears and promises the man that today paradise will be theirs to share. Like the younger son who squandered his inheritance on a life of sin, the criminal beside Jesus "comes to his senses" (Luke 15:17) and begins his journey home to his father's house. The good thief bares his soul and sees God there; he places his trust in Jesus, and is given assurance of his salvation.

As exemplified in the good thief, this represents the essence of what it means to be a Christian. It recognizes the significance of trusting in something greater than one's own self-sufficiency. It overflows in awe at the gift of God who lovingly shares in our suffering and death. It hungers for mercy, and all that it asks is simple remembrance. We are reminded of this each time the Holy Eucharist is celebrated, "*Do this in remembrance of me,*" as Jesus said to those gathered around the table. It acknowledges that without God along with God's mercy, we will be cut off from the presence of God. We see this exemplified in words from the lips of the good thief, "*Remember me....*" to which Jesus responds, "*...truly you will be with me in paradise*" (23:43b). No one else is promised paradise immediately.

What is most amazing is that when Jesus dies, he dies for both thieves. The innocent One dies for those who are guilty, not because they are faithful, but because Jesus is faithful. In a Good Friday sermon Karl Barth reminded his audience, "[Jesus] did not die for the sake of a good world, he died for the sake of an evil world, not for the pious, but for the godless, not for the just, but for the unjust, for the deliverance, the victory and the joy of all, that they may have life" (*Deliverance to the Captives*, Harper & Row, New York, NY., 1961, p. 81). The scandal of the gospel is that those who are saved are not necessarily the spiritually strong and the morally superior. It is those facing what John of the Cross once described as "the dark night of the soul."

Luke makes it clear that the repentant thief's request of Jesus was not a bunch of words that came pouring out of his mouth merely to save his mortal flesh. In an instant he trusted Jesus, and from that we discover what is at the core of Jesus' ministry, the establishment of a meaningful relationship. He is looking beyond the cross at the life that is to follow for the good thief, life eternal with his Lord. When we entrust the details of our lives to God, we need not be surprised at how thoroughly God answers our petitions.

A thief recognizes holiness in the center of his own agony and is promised Jesus' companionship in Paradise---a place, says N.T. Wright, of rest and refreshment before the gift of new life in the resurrection. In the middle of two clashing worldviews Jesus speaks words of forgiveness and commends his life---and death--- to God. Joseph of Arimathea claims a broken body---a labor of love that cannot be repaid. We see in this chaos intimations of a sustaining hope, God's hope at work in the horror and the silence. Luke's passion narrative holds grief and hope together, as indeed these realities are held together in our individual and corporate lives.

Only Luke tells us of the dialogue and the promise to the thief that he would be with Jesus in paradise. He tells us of how Jesus reached out to the poor and all who are on the rough edges of society. Luke tells us of the prodigal son and gives emphasis to moments when exceptionally ill people are healed with the touch of Jesus' hand and words spoken on their behalf. But finally, Luke also addresses Jesus' outreach to the Gentiles. Today we can't help but remember our mortality so that when Easter arrives we can touch the scars in his hands and then remember that death is no longer the end of our stories.

Easter

FROM OBSERVER TO PARTICIPANT

Acts 10:34-43

Theologian Paul Tillich once said, "Christianity is not based on the acceptance of a historical novel; it is based on the witness to the messianic character of Jesus by people who were not interested at all in a biography of the Messiah" (*Systematic Theology*, Vol. II, p. 105). Interestingly, the Resurrection upon which the Christian faith stands or falls, is never explained in the gospels, rather it is recounted detail by detail, what each has witnessed. When Mary Magdalene, Joanna, and Mary the mother of James along with the other women return from the tomb to inform the apostles of their encounter with the two men in dazzling clothes, and that Jesus has been raised from the dead, breathlessly, they tell them that Jesus is somehow alive. The men don't believe this until they encounter the Risen Lord and suddenly realize they are no longer observers but instead have now become participants in this unfolding story that has already begun to radically transform their lives.

In this, his final sermon in Acts, Peter realizes something essential about the God with whom he has already lived in relationship. Peter proclaims what he has seen and believes about Jesus. He is very straight-forward about Jesus' life, death, and resurrection and the importance of all that to the story. But he also emphasizes that the fullness of the story doesn't end with Jesus being raised from the dead. Beginning with Peter's message, the telling and retelling of the story has continued non-stop, and now it comes to us ready to be re-told, not entrusted to a museum, nor a drama caught on camera. Peter assumes his listeners do not know why the good news is so good.

Later the apostle Paul would affirm this in his letter addressed to the church in Corinth, "*If Christ be not raised, your faith is in vain*" (1 Cor. 15:17). But then Paul also mentions being untimely born, but not too late in history to *meet* the Man from Nazareth. For Paul, life began when he encountered the Risen Christ. Likewise, Peter speaks as a participant in the Easter event, a proclamation he emphasizes not to be limited solely to his generation. Each one of us can listen to the Easter story and claim we, too, were born too late, yet, like Paul, are not disqualified from also becoming participants in the drama. The Easter message is not the same as the life after death article we might stumble upon in *Reader's Digest*. This story has many plots, and our life is included as one of those plots. Peter is welcoming us as participants in the community that affirms and celebrates God's reaching out to the world in the Christ event, one which we are surprisingly pulled into.

Exactly how are we participants in the Easter event? In the first place, we recognize that Christ's victory is also our victory. For Christ is risen, *pro nobis*, or in the vernacular, *for us*. As an example, people who work in the front office of a team fortunate enough to win the Super Bowl that year all receive a Super Bowl Ring, even though they weren't at all in the game. Furthermore, they were never even on the playing field, and yet the victory was for them also. Christ rose to convert us, not from earthly life to something beyond life, but from something less than life to the possibility of becoming fully alive, fully what God intended us to be. St. Irenaeus believed that "The glory of God is a human being fully alive." Through the Resurrection God takes delight in us because Easter is not about less death, but more life, not about escape from the grave but escaping the powers of death on earth. It is the power of life entrusted to that which gives us hope in our ability to imagine a tomorrow worth living.

Peter does not make the mistake of making the Easter event into something overly sweet and sentimental. Easter, he believes, represents a demand as well as a promise. We are asked not simply to empathize with the Crucified Christ, but more than that, to pledge our loyalty to the, now, Risen Christ. Following his denial of Jesus, Peter did eventually go the second half by becoming much more than the person he was before Jesus' death. His bold words reveal a very different person from the man we saw a couple of days ago on that fateful night when Peter failed miserably in a critical moment. When the soldiers arrested Jesus Peter went his own way. Three times that night he denied knowing Jesus. But later, when Peter "came to his senses," he wept bitter tears. Somehow Peter became a person whose life was radically transformed after Christ's Resurrection. He became a human being fully alive. Somehow and someway Christ' presence in Peter and the other disciples erupted in a fiery enthusiasm and courage that set the early church on fire.

It is ironic that while Resurrection is the reason for Jesus being Lord of all, what happened on Easter finds its center not in Christ's presence, but on his absence. The discovery of the empty tomb is the heart of the matter for our faith. The first witnesses discover the empty tomb to be a total surprise, something that came while attending to an otherwise routine, if heartbreaking, task. None of the disciples seems fully ready for Easter joy. How difficult and yet all too ordinary. People die all the time. The women who arrive at the tomb are ready for almost anything but what they find. *"Why do you seek the living among the dead?"* asked the dazzling strangers. Have we ever asked that question of ourselves? The women are told, after all, to seek the Risen Christ in the future, in Galilee, where Jesus has gone ahead to carry on his ministry. It is our future brought forward into the present, as N.T. Wright is so apt to remind us. In The Book of Acts we are given further evidence of the resurrection in the ordinary ministries of the church: feeding the hungry, giving hope to the poor, binding up the brokenhearted. Where life overcomes death, that's where we discover evidence of the Risen One.

We need not look at Easter's meaning through the rearview mirror. We stand in the context of a long line of believers who have brought faith forward to us, one generation after another. God has no "grandchildren," only sons and daughters of God. What is it about Easter that brings people to church on Easter? If we aren't convinced or don't have our faith totally intact, then we are still in the story.

Easter confronts our deep-seated fear of death by reminding us that the worst has already been known in our lives. We have confronted death, time and again, and we have risen to new life, life that is on loan from God. Marilyn Adams, Regis Chair of Theology at Oxford University, once observed that the first step to Easter joy is our recognition of the intimacy we share with the power that has been at work in us all along. "Our daily deaths and resurrections," she says, "reassure us that when we come to that big DEADline at the end, we will be dealing with a God Who is experienced at putting Humpty Dumpties back together again" (St. Thomas Church, New Haven, CT). The resurrection, far from being a rather unbelievably happy ending tacked onto the life of Jesus is, for Peter, an indispensable precondition of our telling it. It began not in the tomb but in the *encounter* with the living Lord, which is why we should celebrate Easter not merely as a holiday but as a real event.

A GOD WHO EMPTIES TOMBS

John 20:1-18

Cemeteries typically have few surprises for us. They are very predictable places. John's text takes us into a graveyard, early in the morning while it is still dark. We discover women there, huddled together in the pre-dawn chill, wondering how they can get inside the tomb to anoint the dead body of Jesus. While the women are pondering their next move, the ground around them shakes and an angel appears, his face and clothing a dazzling whiteness. The Roman guards fall to the ground and the women huddle more closely together, fearful, and then a voice is heard, *"Do not be afraid. I know that you are looking for Jesus who was crucified."*

Resurrection is like that. The trouble is we get stuck in the graveyard of this world's ways of doing things and its expectations thrust upon us. In graveyards there's not much to do but remember. Our hope, in the face of the world's death-dealing, stretches no further than rolling away the stone. It takes an earthquake to jolt us into the new and unfamiliar territory of resurrection reality which proclaims, *"He is not here. He is risen."* Risen? What's that?

Author Sandra Cronk in *Dark Night Journey* says, "Stay in the darkness and emptiness. Do not flee from the nothingness or try to fill up that hollow place with your own attempts to create new finite pillars on which to build your life." Easter for Mary Magdalene reveals a God who allows old structures of our lives to break up and begins a work of profound re-patterning in us. The dark night of the Easter story draws us into that empty space where the god we construct disappears, and we are invited to listen to Jesus saying our name from the other side of the resurrection. It is from here the Good News of the Kingdom is to be preached to all people.

But Mary must first let go of things that have shaped how she sees the world, and in the process discover how life is a continual effort of letting go. The world will never be the same; her life will never be the same. In our early years letting go is done eagerly. We let go of crawling in order to walk. We let go of training wheels in order to be free with our newfound sense of balance. We let go of parents as the center of the universe in order to embrace the exciting possibilities of a wider world. We can't wait to let go in order to get on with our lives.

In the latter part of our lives letting go often involves pain and mourning. We let go of our children, we let go of the illusion that time is endless. We let go of unlived dreams. We let go of our health. We bury parents and friends and loved ones. In time we discover that letting go is a paradox. We have to do it if we are to rediscover our lives. We have to do it, and yet, we cannot because we can neither imagine nor do we want a life without that which has been lost. This is the paradox. It is not a problem to be solved; it can only be transcended. We must let go of all we love, keeping faith with Mary that what we let go of will become present to us again in new ways, calling us to new life.

Mary's world had its abundance of darkness. If she didn't believe the world was messed up before, she certainly believed it when Jesus was arrested, mocked, crucified, and buried. She certainly believed it when she showed up at the tomb and discovered the stone rolled away. Somebody stole the body! She doesn't even ask the two disciples what they saw when they looked into the tomb. She doesn't welcome angels with good news to tell and doesn't know Jesus is standing right in front of her. Do you suppose Mary Magdalene told the other disciples the *whole* story, or just those simple words, "*I have seen the Lord!*" In light of what she was expecting to find do you suppose she admitted "I have seen the Lord, but I didn't recognize him at first"? Her own knowledge of Jesus blinded her to the Jesus she never knew because he was who her mind shaped him to be, certainly not a resurrected Jesus.

Mary's dilemma could also be identical to what we face on Easter, the problem of being a citizen of a world with too much darkness and not enough light. In such a case we don't expect much. We can live with a dead Messiah and cling to the idea that this day is really about springtime and the way seeds die and blossom again. Do we really expect anything to come out of it? Do we expect anything to change? We've been going around in circles in the darkness for so long will we know the way out even if the answer is standing right in front of us? Easter shows us how our perspective needs to change. The promise of the gospel is not that we can see Jesus here in the dark, but that Jesus can see us just as he does at the tomb when he called out, "*Mary*"

The shift from looking for Jesus within the small and familiar realm of our own understanding to being met by Jesus in the realm of the resurrection and kingdom reality is not a journey we have ultimate control over. Mary Magdalene was able to wait at the empty tomb, even while she was looking for Jesus as he *had been.* The emptiness is like that; we expect more of the same. But God comes crashing through the darkness of our unbelief, and rolls away the stones which have captivated our limited thinking, and simply says, "*Don't be afraid. I know who you are looking for. He is not here. He is risen.*" God looked down and saw all those graves and said, "Enough!" Although Easter dawns in fear, it refuses to remain there. According to Henri Nouwen, "If we make the 'house of fear' our permanent dwelling, we find our choices narrowed, and our capacity for love constricted until we can hardly breathe" (*Behold the Beauty of the Lord*, p.20).

Whom are we looking for? Are we looking for a Jesus who blesses our way of life, likes the same people we like, and opposes the same people we oppose? Are we looking for a Jesus who condemns other people's sins, but leaves ours unchallenged? Can we see him in the face of people who seem to us to be pretty spectacular sinners?

The question for our Easter faith is quite simply: will we continue to accept him only on our own terms, or will we try to move towards his? When Jesus calls out our name, Mary moves *towards him.* Will we look for him only in the old, familiar places or will we look in the new places as well? Will we react like the soldiers, moving ahead with our plans regardless of what we have learned? Or will we behave like Mary, believing something unexpected that changes everything? Jesus is always going to roll away every stone we have placed to try to keep him in, and will always demand new responses from us, and commitment to a future we have not seen. You may have seen the empty tomb, Mary says, but I have seen the Lord, the one who empties tombs, including mine. An empty tomb is not indicative of an empty life.

LEAVING THE WORLD OF DISAPPOINTMENT

Luke 24:13-35

The women have returned from the tomb to offer their testimony, *"The tomb is empty! He is risen!"* But those listening dismiss it by telling the women it's just an "idle tale." Cleopas and an unnamed follower are heading out of town thinking they had just bet it all on the wrong proverbial horse and lost. They rehash and replay every detail. Jesus was the man and now he's dead and his body has gone missing. It appears they are walking home to resume the life they thought they had left behind. On this road of broken dreams, the incognito Jesus joins their journey, but, as Luke records, *"Their eyes were kept from recognizing him."* They told the stranger, *"We had hoped that he was the one who would redeem Israel!"* Could they have missed something? Is possible they have misunderstood the Jesus they had known?

It takes little imagination to see ourselves in the story; we fall into a spiritual black hole and everything we believe suddenly evaporates. For them it's the death of their friend. For any one of us it could be a death, an experience of loss or disillusion, a betrayal or personal failure. The two travelers are lost, rudderless and without much hope, and so full of doom and gloom that they fail to register the sign of hope that comes up and walked along with them. They're stuck in the muck of their own story. Do we, too, get stuck in our own interpretation of the story?

Whether we acknowledge it or not, Sunday after Sunday Christ is in our midst as we worship. Day by day the Spirit of God accompanies each of us. But often our "eyes are kept from recognizing" God with us, among us, in us. Rather than telling these two disciples that they were blind, Jesus enters into their world and understanding. "What are you discussing with each other?" "How's it going with you two?" The two grieving disciples are surprised that this stranger Jesus is clueless about "the things that have taken place," and he responds by drawing them out, "What things?"

It is this open-ended question---one which cannot be answered with a simple "yes" or "no"---that invites us to bring our stories to the surface. Sometimes the narrative we hear from persons seems more mundane than the earth-shaking events these two disciples are relating. Kathleen Norris in her book, "*Dakota: A Spiritual Geography* (Houghton Mifflin, 1993, p. 76) says, even gossip "is theology translated into experience. In it we hear great stories of conversion. At its deepest level, small-town gossip is about how we face matters of life and death."

As the journey to Emmaus progresses Jesus talks too, just like they wanted---or thought they did. Perhaps the combination of mind-numbing miles and his words were just the thing to keep them from falling completely down the rabbit hole. But as Luke tells it, ultimately it isn't the road-talk that turns their thinking around. It is something much simpler. It's a gesture at the table. Breaking the bread; *that* was what did it. Not the voice. Not the face. Not the scripture recital or the theology lesson or the prophetic commentary. It is the bread in his hands. That I how they know it is Jesus. Just listening to their pain he understands exactly what they need---on the road to Emmaus, when the disciples are finally ready to sit down to supper---to see beyond themselves, to see Jesus. Though Jesus was present with them long before they recognized him, because the two travelers were living the story from the script of their own expectations and disappointments, they were unable to see outside of that story.

We are not immune from such experiences. We tend to see what we're looking for and not see what we aren't looking for. We selectively pay attention to the experiences in our lives, noticing those events that fit our expectations and meanings, for they are the ones we build into our lives, the ones that become true for us. Those that don't fit our expectations often get lost. Our familiar and certain stories close our eyes to the unexpected and, thus the unexpected is lost to us. Their eyes aren't opened, and recognition (new thinking) doesn't happen until they find themselves living in a completely new story, Jesus' presence at their table. In that experience they are living a new story in which their old story has no place. How might we loosen our grip on the certainties of our faith stories so that our expectation make room for God's novelty?

The two disciples do not just sit and revel in their new spiritual awareness. Rather, they get up and head back to Jerusalem with a newly-found courage that allows them to brave the dangers of the travel and the exhaustion of a long day, to re-join the other disciples. They must do so because the story is to be a shared story that directs their lives in communion with others, and not a story of personal spiritual insight.

Though we come each Sunday to our place of worship, it is easy to miss Christ because, in part, we forget that Christ comes not because we make it so, but because it is Christ's church. Granted, we are there to offer our best to God, but we do so understanding that nothing we do---tympani, trumpets, trombones---will coerce Christ into our presence. Christ comes as a gift. Just like the two dis-spirited disciples, Jesus comes suddenly out of nowhere. We will miss such sacred moments if we do not look with more than our eyes and listen with more than our ears. If we seek God with our hearts and souls, we may catch a glimpse. Listen for God in a phrase from a hymn, a word from scripture, a word of hope during prayer, in the breaking of the bread. While our encounter with God may be for but a moment, we must always remind ourselves that the God we worship is present with us for the whole journey.

Each time we make our way to receive the Eucharist let this journey be our Emmaus, where we come with our defeats and discouragements, our own failures of kindness or generosity, our doubts and our faithlessness, and recognize the risen Christ among us in a broken loaf and a cup poured out. When we recognize our own risen Lord---not only in the broken Bread but in the breaking heart---it is then that Easter dawns for us in all its realism. I am certainly glad that his being alive doesn't depend on our ability to understand how Jesus operates. We keep on loving the wrong things, chasing after the wrong dreams, licking our own selfish wounds. And he keeps walking up behind us. Did not our hearts burn this morning as the scriptures were opened up to us?

LIFE AFTER EASTER

Luke 21:1-19

Richard Foster, according to an article that appeared in the *New York Times* a few years ago, approaches the Bible with the recommendation that believers "live the experience" as they read the gospel text. In other words, are we still breathing in the refreshing air of Easter or are we back to our old routine way of life again? Perhaps this is why Jesus needed to appear to his disciples repeatedly over the span of roughly forty days. These post-resurrection stories are not just another way of giving us more evidence of the resurrection, but instead proclaim a beginning. Had Jesus not come and spent time with them after the resurrection it's not likely the disciples would have had the courage to risk their lives proclaiming the gospel in Jerusalem and beyond.

One way to understand this appearance is to see his resurrection as the way for them to really come alive. Perhaps, then, they could avoid the temptation to fall into "life as usual" but also catch a glimpse of how the Christian life looks. Jesus catches the disciples doing what they were quite familiar with, that of fishing. The text from John tells us they fished all night long, caught nothing, and grew more frustrated with each passing hour. Unrecognized by the disciples, Jesus speaks to them from the shore, saying, "*Have you caught any fish?*" Already knowing the answer, Jesus tells them to toss the net back into the water. As the fishermen struggle with the payload of fish caught in their net, they realize that this stranger giving orders from a distance is actually Jesus. The enormity of the catch affords Jesus the opportunity to share with them a meal of fish and bread as a reminder of his sustaining presence. Slowly they are drawn nearer to the One who first loved them. How can they now possibly return to the emptiness of the former life that is no longer the same in light of God's raising Jesus from the dead?

Philip Melanchthon, friend of Martin Luther, once wrote, "This is to know Christ; to know his benefits." The writer of John's Gospel wants to show us the benefits, and how the Resurrection happened in this world, not in some spectral, shadowy existence. Jesus is not the projection of wish-fulfillment. He is real. He stands on the beach. He speaks to the disciples across the water. He instructs them where to catch fish. Jesus' disciples thought when he was taken from them that all wonder and delight had gone out of their lives. Jesus meets his friends in the hour of their need and despair.

The fire for the breakfast is not the only one Jesus lights. He also lights a fire under Peter. In reading John's narratives it's wise to pay attention to peter. He's a good barometer for helping us gain greater insight into what is really going on. This text from John's Gospel is no exception. Perhaps that's why after Jesus' friends finished eating it is Peter to whom Jesus directs his questions. Jesus, as we recall, has unfinished business to address with Peter. From the moment of Peter's denial of Jesus up to this moment of deep questioning by Jesus, Peter's life has been a dark one. The unfortunate instance in the courtyard a few nights before placed him under a dark cloud. Only afterwards did he realize the temerity of his actions toward the betrayed Jesus. His life from then to this moment was just a matter of going through the motions. There was also a part of Peter that died and now it is time for Jesus to address that with him.

Jesus asks Simon Peter three times what appears to be the same question, *"Simon, Son of John, do you love me more than these?"* Simon Peter responds, *"Yes, Lord, you know that I love you."* Two slight variations of Jesus' question follow, and Simon Peter's response is always the same. Three questions correspond to three denials, both over a charcoal fire reminiscent of a few nights ago. Jesus chooses his words carefully. When Peter replies the word he uses for "love" is different to the one Jesus uses in the first two questions. The third time Jesus uses the word Peter himself had been using.

Each of Peter's answers is followed by a fresh command, a new commission from Jesus. "Feed my lambs.....Tend my sheep.....Feed my sheep." Not only is Jesus trusting Peter to return to fruitful work, he is sharing his own work, his own ministry, with Peter. Jesus already has fish on the grill when he asks them to bring some of their own. He didn't really need theirs, but Jesus wants them to share in his ministry. We can also interpret Jesus' three-fold questioning of Peter as Jesus' way of reminding him that one can never, as someone once suggested, "out-deny" Jesus. No matter how many times we reject Jesus, he is always moving towards us, no matter what.

This encounter is commonly referred to as the "reinstatement" of Peter. But in light of the transformation that occurs in Peter, this can also be Peter's resurrection from the dead. How could Peter possibly return to the self-deception and emptiness of the old life that is no longer the same in light of God's raising Jesus from the dead? Peter would no longer drift alone on a barren sea worried about coming up empty-handed, nothing to show for hours of relentless and frustrating work. No longer would he have to fret about having enough. The net they hauled in with the incredible number and variety of fish never breaks. Jesus had a heart for the tired and disappointed fishermen by coming to them on the shore of the lake because that is where they live and work, and that's where he comes to us. When Jesus told them, *"Drop your nets on the right side of the boat,"* he made it convenient because the fish were right under their noses.

There are some obvious conclusions one could draw from Peter's encounter. The first is that Resurrection happens to us in the real world. The Gospel happens and has its power to have an influence on us in the physical world. There is no need to "spiritualize" the Resurrection as something that has its fullest meaning only when we die. It means the renewal of life, not an escape from it.

The Resurrection often manifests itself the way that it happened to the disciples, in their hour of disappointment, frustration, hopelessness, and doubt, when they "have caught nothing." When we have given up on our own attempts at trying to save ourselves and abandoned the fantasy of an uncluttered world, the Resurrection breaks into our lives with transforming power to help us live above the cluttered plane of life.

Those who have love for Jesus are best positioned to see his Resurrection power at work. The unbroken net of Jesus' love is the net holding us up, placing him in the present and involving him in the difficulties and hopes of the moment. Don't give up five minutes before the miracle!

HOPE IN THE NOT YET

Acts 1:6-14

Acts of the Apostles is Luke's second book, following on the aftermath of his gospel. While the gospel provides vivid details surrounding Jesus' birth, life, death, and resurrection, Luke found it necessary to tell us what happened after Jesus was raised from the dead. It is called Acts of the *Apostles* (emphasis mine) because it is not centered exclusively on Jesus, but on the events that surrounded the apostles. One of the first events Luke records is Jesus' dramatic ascension into heaven from atop the Mount of Olives overlooking Jerusalem.

Of all the answers Christ gave to the many questions posed to him, one of the most frustrating must have been his response to the disciples' query, *"Lord, is this the time when you will restore the kingdom to Israel?"* (v. 6). They had been on a spiritual roller coaster, going from hope to devastation, from joy to terror, but then, in the aftermath, they heard baffling reports of Christ's being alive, which struck them as being nothing but *"an idle tale"* (Luke 24:11) until Jesus himself stood among them. Certainly by now their lives could settle down with a bit more certainty and assurance that their future will not be a repeat of the past, that the coming days will be stable and predictable. When they asked the resurrected Jesus if this was the time when he will restore Israel's kingdom, nothing would have been more satisfying than a clear and simple "Yes!" Instead, Christ tells them such knowledge is not theirs to know as he prepares to disappear into a cloud! Before they can catch their breath, Jesus is gone. The Spirit has not come. The church is left between their memories of the past and the promise for the future.

What kind of a religion is it in which the faithful appear regularly abandoned by their God? In his book, *A Grief Observed*, in which C.S. Lewis talks about the death of his wife, he writes, "Talk to me about the duty of religion, and I'll listen gladly. Talk to me about the duty of religion and I'll listen submissively. But don't come talking to me about the consolations of religion or I shall suspect that you don't understand." Heaven's all right for those who are there, but what about us? Must we get on with Jesus' work without him?

While the ascension is the end of Jesus' visible presence on earth, it is at the same time a new beginning, a new era for his followers. The angels who spoke to the disciples on the Mount of Olives---who by this time had their hearts in their throats---were in essence saying that what remained of Jesus remained in them, that what they needed and knew of Jesus they still had. They had now become the very animated, flesh and blood, body of Christ. They would find him and know him present again within their experience as they pushed out, left home, and went to Samaria and to the ends of the earth. That's where they would see Jesus.

I recall a similar feeling of striking out on my own when I was dropped off at college to begin my freshman year. There was a sense that when my folks bid me farewell that September day, the goodbye had an ominous feel to it. It was different from those short out-of-town excursions I had taken many times before. It was as if *this* goodbye was for keeps. Even though I knew then that I would be returning home for holidays and summer breaks, from that day forward, home, for me, was out there somewhere in the offing waiting for me to discover for myself. And so, this "finding home" wherever, within themselves or in the world, must have been what dampened the disciple's spirits as Jesus left them when he ascended into heaven. He was prodding them out and on their way, which in retrospect is what was happening to me while I gazed at my parent's car going away towards what had been my home for several years.

For the disciples they would go on to discover Jesus' presence again and again. But it was this *leaving* that was the occasion for their real growth, and indeed, mine also. Sometimes insight only comes when the props and supports are knocked out from under us, when we are left alone without wishing to be so. That's the way it was for the disciples. It was only as Jesus turned the disciples loose with whatever he had given them up to that point that they would come to know what he had given them and who they actually were. Those first followers of Jesus were forced to let go of Jesus as he ascended. They didn't know what to do next, but nevertheless, they would soon discover in his leaving, in being left alone, that they had found his presence more obvious in his absence. *Then* they were emboldened to go forth and be his witnesses to the end of the earth.

I believe for all time that God is here with us in ourselves and in our world, ready to do more with our lives than we could ever imagine or think possible. And painful though the losses and endings may be, perhaps they are a sign of new possibilities being born, the occasions for God's breaking into our lives in new ways. That is what having faith in the not-yet means, for "waiting time" is not purely passive. It is not empty time or downtime. Waiting time, as someone once said, is when we become more authentically human because we manage to give up the illusion that we possess powers that in truth belong only to God.

It is to our advantage that Jesus leaves us and ascends to his Father, for now he is no longer bound by time and space. Now he no longer belongs just to that little bewildered band of disciples in Palestine. Now his ministry is not just to the lost sheep of Israel, and his power is not limited to geography and clock. We are not left desolate and alone because Christ's presence follows us always. He is acquainted with all our ways, as Psalm 139 reminds us, "*Where can I go from your Spirit? Where can I flee from your presence?*" (v. 7).

For author Philip Yancey the Ascension represents his greatest single struggle of faith. What he wrestles with is not whether it happened or not, nor even how it happened, but why it happened. "Would it not have been better," he asks, "if the Ascension had never happened? If Jesus had stayed on earth he could answer our questions, solve our doubts, mediate our disputes of doctrine and polity" (*The Jesus I Never Knew*, Zondervan, 1995, p.229).

To celebrate the Ascension is to recognize it as a moment that, as with the disciples, embraces an explicit memory which becomes our fervent hope. And by so doing, when the realm of God dawns among us, forever or for a moment, we will recognize it. We will know it because some have lived it. We will confirm it because we have dreamed it. We will mark and name it because we are an expectant people, laboring to give lives of witness, waiting, watching, wondering, bound to the particular memory of Jesus' love and teeming with God's pregnant hope.

Pentecost

THE HOLY SPIRIT FOR TODAY

Acts 2:1-21

We live in a power-conscious age. We use terms like "power-play" in sports, of "power politics" in international affairs. We are aware of the power of wealth, the power of publicity. But Pentecost celebrates a different kind of power because it's not something we generate. As Acts tells us, the Holy Spirit came on the day of Pentecost to empower the disciples and "devout Jews from every nation" who were assembled in Jerusalem. They *"began to speak in other languages, as the Spirit gave them ability"* (2:4). This is the fulfillment of Jesus' command and promise that the disciples would "receive power" when the Holy Spirit came upon them.

Because we are a consumer-driven and technologically saturated world, in many ways this power seems to have been drained of all mystery. The Holy Spirit is too often the forgotten factor in the world and in the church today. At various points in history, the church has been tempted to live by its own power, fully confident of its own resources as it plans its mission. It "stumbles" because it cannot see beyond its own resources. The church lacked power before Pentecost, but once it came, God's mission through the church would not be stopped. Today we wonder how that Spirit of Pentecost can possibly mean as much for us today as it did for the disciples in Jerusalem. But while it may not consist of new information, it does equip the church to live faithfully in the midst of new situations. But we dare not attempt to mimic the Holy Spirit.

A story is told about a traveling evangelist who always put on a grand finale at his revivals. When he was to preach at the church, he would secretly hire a small boy to hide in the balcony with a dove in a cage. Toward the end of his sermon, the preacher would shout for the Holy Spirit to come down, and the boy hidden above would dutifully release the dove. At one revival meeting, however, nothing happened when the excited preacher called for the Holy Spirit to descend. He again raised his arms and exclaimed, "Come down, Holy Spirit!" Still there no sign of the dove. The preacher then heard the anxious voice of the small boy call down from above, "Sir, a yellow cat just ate the Holy Spirit. Shall I throw down the yellow cat?"

As the disciples try to make sense of what Jesus is telling them, he provides reassurance. Before sending the mighty rush of wind of the Holy Spirit Jesus tells them, "*I will not leave you desolate.*" In whatever new situation they find themselves, they will not be left solely to their own devices. Power is never achieved when it is pursued for itself as Dr. Stanley Jones made note of in his autobiography, "The Holy Spirit has been the working force in my life........ A power not mine has been and is working in and through me" (*A Song of Ascents*). Jesus won't abandon them, but he does indeed give them something to do when he tells them, "*You shall receive power when the Holy Spirit comes upon you and you shall be my witnesses*" (Lk 24:49).

The image of clothing is a good illustration to help us comprehend that sense of the Holy Spirit's power "coming upon us." In today's every-day world we discover how clothing often connotes power. Queen Elizabeth is clothed with power when she puts on her robes of state. Judges are clothed with power when they wear their robes. The Bible has similar examples. Aaron was clothed with power when he arrayed himself in his high-priestly garments. In the book of Judges we read, "*The Spirit of the Lord clothed himself with Gideon.*" Elisha was clothed with power when he put on the mantle that had fallen from the shoulders of Elijah. Jesus was clothed with power as the woman with the issue of blood discovered when the thrill of health flashed through her as she touched the tassel of his robes.

The latter part of our reading from Acts contains a line of prophesy from Joel. "*In those last days I'll pour out my Spirit on all flesh"* (2:17a). There's an interesting anomaly here. On Pentecost, the crowd gathered not because there was a wind, but because there was *"the sound of wind."* When the sound of that wind raised eyebrows, people from throughout the Roman Empire who spoke different languages and possessed different dialects immediately took flight. Interestingly, though, it was not to the Jewish courtroom, the Sanhedrin, or the quarters of Pontius Pilate. Instead, they made their way to an upper room to inquire of God the nature of this sound. The message here is that the Church is establish by God so that when the world is unclear, unsure, uncertain, God's house is the location where we gain insight about the holy mysteries of the universe. Beneath the wide umbrella of God's house the dying can live. Those who wait upon the Lord can renew their strength. Jesus gives them a hope-filled future.

The arrival of Pentecost couldn't have come any sooner. The shock they had experienced in the days leading up to Pentecost still reverberated deep within them. To them the Cross was a disaster and the resurrection a mystery. Theirs was a lost leader and a cause that had collapsed. The future they were counting on was gone. The dream, or a hope or a possibility had in a matter of days vanished. Whenever we experience the loss of what some refer to as a "future story," it can feel like we've not only lost the dream, but the future itself no longer has the feel of an invitation. There's no longer a narrative out there for us to latch onto.

Writing about "future stories" and how they create meaning for our lives, Andy Lester says people live their lives in three time frames---past, present, and future---and each time-frame informs and makes meaningful the other two. It is the dynamic interplay between these three that forms the context of meaningful life narratives. Ultimately, he suggests, all of our future stories are fragile and will fall apart. We reach goals we have set and not looked beyond; we lose our health; we retire from careers; we lose loved ones. Consequently, he says, our future stories have to be grounded in something more. Ultimately, our hope has to rest in a future that God carries and anticipates with us (*Hope in Pastoral Care and Counseling*). Pentecost created infinite possibilities for all future stories and the promise of God's power of the Holy Spirit for all time.

Within God's promise even our broken stories can find meaning and continuity, *nevertheless*. We may live in difficult times; *nevertheless*, God is guiding this world through the pains to a future fulfillment of promise. The Spirit is not always as visibly active in the church as we might desire; *nevertheless*, the Spirit is unceasingly attentive to our pleading, even to the point of bringing our prayers home to God when we are unable to articulate them for ourselves. We may not know what God has in store for the Church; *nevertheless*, the Spirit knows the mind of God and leads us toward the will of the One who made us for God's own future story.

A PEACE THAT STRIKES HOME

John 20:19-23

A key dynamic throughout John's gospel is the question of whether people will recognize who Jesus truly is. It begins with the tragic note in the first chapter that "*the world came into being through him, yet the world did not know him*" (1:10). It plays out in Nathaniel's excited confession, "*You are the Son of God...*" (1:49), in Nicodemus' inadequate appraisal of Jesus, "*Rabbi, we know you are a teacher who has come from God.*"(3:2). There is also the growing awareness of the Samaritan woman and the man born blind (chpts. 4 and 9). The theme of recognition has come to a climax with Mary's recognition of the risen Jesus (20:16), and now the disciples join her in Easter faith, in seeing the risen Lord.

The text says the disciples are huddled behind locked doors because they are in a state of fear when suddenly Jesus comes unexpectedly into the presence of a weary band of dispirited disciples. Embodying the tenacious and compassionate grace of God, he breaks through their locked doors of cynicism and disillusionment and fear with the words," *"Peace be with you,"* the traditional mid-Eastern greeting which means: "May God give you every good thing."

It is significant that the first word is "peace" rather than "forgiveness," a surprise, for sure, considering their recent behavior. Christ does not offer an easy way out of the regret and sorrow the disciples must have for their fear, and in Peter's case, denial. Peace does not eradicate the need to come to terms with their faithlessness. Peace empowers them to face what has happened and how they reacted. Peace makes it possible for them to bear the sight of Christ's wounds and to consider the implication of those wounds for the ministry they will now undertake.

Scott Bader-Saye reveals in his book, *Following Jesus in a Culture of Fear,* how our drive for security rules our lives. "When we fear excessively we live in a mode of---reacting to and plotting against---evil rather than actively seeking and doing what is good and right. Our overwhelming fears need to be overwhelmed by bigger and better things" (Brazos Press, 2007). This is precisely Jesus' approach to his disciples.

Jesus could have just risen and gone straight back to heaven. But he lingers, he appears, if only to reveal to the disciples these bigger and better things. Unimpeded by the locked doors and in the midst of their heightened anxiety Jesus offers them his peace---every good thing from God. Peace is what fearful people never have. Peace is not something we can attain solely on our own no matter what safeguards we put in place. It is a gift of God, impossible apart from God's personal presence. Jesus follows this greeting by showing them his hands and side. While we may think of our heavenly existence as perfect, all troubles left behind, Jesus still has scars; they were not blotted out by the resurrection. Nothing better defined his character. It is as if he bore those scars from then and through all eternity. The hurt of the cross is still palpable. That is what he wants them to have---to have peace.

Such a gracious offer can easily trigger a quandary in their minds about how they, in the future, would be able to address the rupture of their relationships with others, especially if they are not at a place in their lives where they can forgive. Perhaps this is precisely what many of us wrestle with too. It may be that forgiveness is not yet even appropriate. Nevertheless, it brings into focus the larger issue of what it would mean to live the pattern of the risen Christ, to start with hope of wholeness for that person, which is what Jesus sought for his disciples. A greeting of peace would not be a way of saying, "It's all over and done with and I forgive you." Rather the blessing would be an expression of our holiest dream for the other person that he or she could come to terms with what they had done and be transformed. Our greeting of peace would not be the cessation of the tensions in the relationship. Peace would mean the re-alignment, a re-figuring of those tensions so that our relationship might be made new, just as the relationship of the resurrected Jesus and the disciples is made new by the peace that he offers to them.

Resurrection is more than something that happened way back when. Resurrection for us today is a pattern of renewal that begins with the blessing of peace. It is a dynamic peace that gives our quaking hearts the stability th ey need to view the wounds, to realize that scars of injustice and violence never completely disappear. But in any event we will at least discover what "Christ is risen" really means for us personally.

A most enduring moment in the resurrection stories comes when, as John records, "[Jesus] *breathed on them and said, 'Receive the Holy Spirit.'"* To breathe on someone you have to be very close to them. For us to be breathed upon by Jesus we have to get close to Jesus. This is the same brea th God used to cr eate Adam. God breathed into some mortal insubs tantial mud of the earth the very divine breath of life. To thes e disciples, their hope having evaporated and shivering in fear, Jesus breaths on them, and creates new life, actually new pe ople. They become as new as Adam on the first day of his first week.

This holy breath, the rush of wind that wafted over the nothingness, created the universe. It is the same breath of God that caused the dead and washed up bones to rise up, take on flesh, and become a new people (Ezekiel 37). It is the sigh we feel when we do not know how to pray, but it is the Spirit praying within us with, as Paul reminds us, " *sighs too deep for words"* (Rom. 8:26). The Church is not just an institution that looks to the past for its origins, but an event of God's Spirit constituted as a fresh start every time, in every Eucharist when the priest calls down the Holy Spirit to bless and sanctify everyday bread and wine to become the body and blood of Jesus. Emory professor Fred Craddock says that "without Pentecost, Easter offers us a risen Christ whose return to glory leaves the church to face the world armed with nothing but fond memories of how it once was when Jesus was here" (*Preaching Through the Christian Year,* Trinity Press Int., 1992, 298.)

Neither death nor door locks prevent Jesus from commissioning his followers. By breathing on his disciples, Jesus doesn't simply impart to them a super power. As the Resurrected One, he resurrects their faith with his life-giving Spirit. Mission, as John shows us, begins not with the church but with God, and in particular, God's peace.

FAITH FOR THE LONG HAUL

Hebrews 11:29-12:2

New Testament scholar Robert Jewett describes the book of Hebrews as a "letter to pilgrims." They are people on a mission. Today's reading, which is midway through Hebrews 11, opens with that great roll call of the Old Testament faithful. The writer mentions the faith that carried the people across the Red Sea, faith that brought down the walls of Jericho, the faith of Rahab, Gideon, Samson, David and the prophets. Faith is defined earlier as *"the assurance of things hoped for, the conviction of things not seen,"* a reminder to us that the heroes and heroines of Hebrew history *expected* great things from God. An old American folk song says, "We don't know where we're going, but we're on our way." That wasn't the case with the Hebrews because they knew precisely where they were headed. For them, the axial moment of salvation history was a hope, powerfully held but only dimly apprehended, which drew them *forward.*

For centuries, since the adoption of Christianity as the state religion by the Roman emperor and up through the Second World War, the existence of God was a well-established fact of our culture. All life was structured around God. But it's different now; new kinds of churches, with a new kind of music and a new way of presenting the gospel story. In some ways, we are closer to the situations of the heroes of faith in the book of Hebrews than we are to those of our fathers and mothers a generation ago. Maybe this is why the book of Hebrews sounds so winsomely modern to our ears. We can identify with its theme and spirit. We, too, are trying to make our way through absurd surroundings to a place where things make more sense to us. We, too, are caught up in the conundrum of faith. We, too, may occasionally wonder if God really does exist and if we are indeed following in the way that leads to truth and life.

But we twenty-first century pilgrims differ from our Old Testament ancestors in that we believe that in the life, death, and resurrection of Jesus the ancient hope has been fulfilled. We are privileged to look backward to *that* fulfillment, keeping its memory fresh and alive in our worship. History's direction has been disclosed to us, but its consummation is still to come, which is why we can still learn something from our ancestors. The book of Hebrews draws upon the image of a race, how the faithful persevere surrounded by what the writer calls "*a great cloud of witnesses.*"

Church historian Martin Marty tells of one of his seminary professors who had a tremendous impact on generations of students. Reflecting on this professor's life at his memorial service, it was said, "We did not climb the stairs to his office to hear the answer, but to see it." There are those who act as a great cloud of witnesses for us. The walls and ceiling of Eastern Orthodox Churches are covered with glowing icons, which, beyond being merely ornamental, have the effect of reminding worshipers that the saints are *really* there. Abraham, the great sojourner, Sarah, the mother of a future pillar of the faith, Paul, transformed from persecutor to gospel globetrotter. If we examine how each of them made their way through all the twists and turns of life, we'll see how their becoming so entangled in the existence of God led them to the discovery that even moments of doubt and struggle become part of the overall picture of faith development and a brighter understanding of the ways of God.

When we enter a church it's likely we not only feel the presence of God, but also own *great cloud of witnesses* who have gone before us. Often during funeral services I notice people gazing up at the ceiling as if recalling the great cloud of witnesses who long ago made an impression on them. In May of 1954, Englishman Roger Bannister became the first to run the mile in under four minutes. In the first year following Bannister's feat, thirty-seven other runners broke the four-minute mile. Today, more than five hundred have run the mile in under four minutes. Roger Bannister broke the barrier, and others have followed. Likewise, Jesus broke another barrier that transformed the world. His act is one of prevenient grace, going before us before we are even aware that we need it, as " *the pioneer and perfecter of our faith*" (12:2).

In Hebrews 12:1 it says, " *...let us run with perseverance the race marked out for us.*" I, for one, am delighted the author chose that word because not all of us care to sprint through life. The word that is translated as "perseverance" can also be rendered as "patient endurance." If we're going to finish the race, we need to rely on patient endurance. Singin g even in the darkest midnight; praying fervently until the blessing comes; shouting "Hallelujah," even when heartache is on the ho rizon; handling our grief with grace; keeping our cool when the he at is on; generously giving our tithes and offerings even when there is more month than money and the next paycheck seems a million miles away----patient endurance. Patient endurance woul d not be necessary if life was a sprint, but since life can be experienced at times as a grueling marathon, patient endu rance is a prerequisi te. One does not develop an attitude of patience na turally. Ironically, the only way to gain patience is by showing patience.

Our text is a prescient reminder that we come out of the clouds by faith. By faith we see. By faith we cross the great divides. By faith the people of God come to our true selves. Faith is a form of spiritual courage. Faith is belief in the next page, in the fifteenth chance, the light around the corner. The term, "inner fortitude" has come to mean for many of us as a way of describing religious gutsiness. As we age, we get strong from the inside out. We may not even know our full courage, but it's all there, just waiting to come out from under its scars. God teaches us to dance as though no one is looking, love as if we have never been hurt, and work--- as a bumper sticker said---as though we didn't need the money.

Much like our biblical ancestors listed on the great roll, the older we get, the more responsibility we have. Our children may have left home but our links to them have not. We may attend more funerals than weddings but that doesn't mean we don't have a sense of the fresh and the new. In the words of writer Donna Schaper, "Our bodies may be acti ng funny but it doesn't mean we don't enjoy them." When we th ink of all the patriarchs and people of faith---ancient and near---who have gone before us, we can believe in what is coming, faithfully, as much as we believe in what has already been. The God who brought the likes of Abraham, Sarah, Paul, Peter, and Barnabas, continues to bring such folk into our midst. We stay faithful best by leaning into the future to find out just what new and good thing God is going to do next. We endure what we have to endure. And if we believe our Bibles, then by faith, we know it is coming.

IT'S BAD NEWS BEFORE GOOD NEWS

Luke 15:1-10

Luke's text provides us with stories of the Lost and Found. In his classic definition, Frederick Buechner says, "The Gospel is bad news before it is good news." He reminds us that we face this news when we look into the mirror; there we are. The Gospel is, of course, also good news because, despite our shortcomings and frailties, we are loved by God anyway, cherished, forgiven, bleeding, but also, as Buechner says, "bled for" (*Telling the Truth*, Harper, 1977).

One of the most striking features in the twin parables of The Lost Sheep and The Lost Coin is how each resonates with our state of being. The sheep and coins don't repent. They don't come to their senses and turn around and make a new start on their own. They don't find themselves; they are found. Likewise, we are saved by grace and not by our half-baked, quasi-successful efforts at repentance. Luke's narrative implies that God actively seeks us when we have wondered away. God accomplishes this often through other people, in "coincidental" encounters---a chance word, a silent example, or even a negative example which brings home to us how barren life can be without God. The sheep has wondered off. The world has led them astray, and now they are bleating for help on some forsaken ledge. But they are moved when they hear how the good shepherd has left all the others in order to find them.

Becoming unknowingly among the lost, though, is not the situation of a good many congregations today. Most of the lost we know have to be convinced they are lost. Most are looking to find themselves, thinking they will be saved if they can find their true selves. Consequently, they become the seekers, not the lost. But, as the parables remind us, no one can, by searching, find God, at least not until we get to the place where we hear God's convicting voice and feel the collapse of our own proud efforts. What we once failed to achieve by will, we might now receive by grace; for it is the fundamental insight of the Gospel that we do not find God, God finds us in the fog of our lost-ness.

The story of the lost sheep is not only about us as individuals, but there is a salvific corporate dimension as well. When we read this parable we often keep our eye solely on Jesus' pursuit of the one lost sheep. But there's also meaning that accompanies the other ninety-nine. How has the absence of one of their own affected them? The shepherd goes after the lost sheep not only to save her, but more importantly, to save the other ninety-nine. The other ninety-nine cannot achieve wholeness apart from the hundredth. A careful scrutiny of the text will reveal to us that there is no individual salvation or blessedness—no rugged individualism, no rejection of the vulnerable. The majority cannot be saved apart from the well-being of the minority. This is God's wisdom, which confounds the wisdom that colors our own personal interests. Jesus' interest is embracing all of us, body, mind, and spirit, for any of us to be whole.

Likewise, discovering the lost coin is essential to the completion of the other nine coins. The many are incomplete without the one. This one, however, is not lost by choice, or careless wandering, but by being caught in the cracks. Questions that prick our social conscience come to mind. How many persons are lost because no one notices, no one cares, no one offers support or welcome? Bruce Epperly, commenting on this text says, "A healthy society or church does not abandon anyone---no child is truly left behind in the inner city of rural Appalachia. The church is called to a style of hospitality that seeks rather than waits, that goes out to find the lost rather than expecting them to come to church" (*Patheos.com*, 9-12-10). We are reminded that the church doors are open to let us *out*. Our salvation and wholeness depend on the lost being found and the homeless welcomed. In the story of the sheep and the coin, the punch line in each case depends on the Jewish belief that the two halves of God's creation, heaven and earth, were meant to fit together and be in harmony with each other. If we discover what's going on in heaven, we'll discover how things were meant to be on earth; " *Thy kingdom come on earth as in heaven,*" is what we say in the Lord's Prayer.

Author Wallace H. Kirby shares the story of an inner city church where a large corporation was offering them a great deal of money for their site to build a parking lot. The money would be sufficient for them to move to another location and serve more people. Though exciting, there wa s resistance, reminders of this church's many years as a guardian of a building with great historical significance. Ultimately they sold the site and moved. For its pastor the decision was between being a museum or being in mission, staying and glorying in their past and serving few people, or giving up their past and gearing themselves to abundant ministry among the city's people. They opted for mission, into what their hearts to ld them would be a challenging, and yet, very fulfilling future (*If Only*, CSS Publishing).

According to Luke, the Pharisees and scribes came down on the side of a museum religion, directing their efforts towards those who were stable, pious and not a liability if invited into the country club. They preferred synagogue programs for the dependable, like-minded types. But Jesus disappointed them by insisting that the call was one of mission: reaching out to those who needed great mercy. Paying attention to these "lost" persons would, of course, change the comfortable fellowship the scribes and Pharisees enjoyed at the synago gue, to say nothing of putting a dent into its budget.

Such is the character of God: it is his good pleasure that the lost should be redeemed because they are God's children. Their wanderings have caused him pain and God rejoices over their return home. It is the "redemptive joy" of God of which Jesus speaks; the joy in forgiving. Being found by God changes everything. Being loved by God into repentance turns us around, reestablishes our position, rewrites our address. The story takes all that we call holy and righteous and worthy of honor and pulls the rug out from under it. The story takes all that we call hopeless, worthless, and unlovable, and redeems it with a love that, quite frankly, baffles us.

The real challenge of these parables is for us challenge those whom we encounter to ask the questions to which stories like these are the answer. But also, to give us the chance to tell stories about finding something that was lost.

CLAIMING THE HIGH GROUND

Luke 13:10-17

When our oldest daughter was learning to drive I was sitting next to her as we drove along a four-lane residential street. Ahead of us down the road was parked a large utility truck. As we got closer I suggested she change lanes, to which she replied, "I can't change lanes. I'm within 500 feet of an intersection!" This incident raises the question as to whether this is a lesson in perfect obedience to the law or about learning to be a safe driver. The answer to such philosophical questions rests in our willingness to do what Jesus did, claim the high ground. In his book, *The Divine Conspiracy*, Dallas Willard suggests that in some churches, the Christian faith has been reduced to "sin management," doing wrong and being wrong.

It is this mindset that we observe in Luke's text gospel for which Jesus is readily criticized for a Sabbath-day healing of a woman who has been crippled for eighteen years. A few centuries before this incident, the synagogue movement had grown up in an era when the temple was no longer the center of Israel's corporate life. God's presence among the people was experienced through diligent observance of "the Law." Such rigid preoccupation with Sabbath observance was operative in the early Christian community to whom Luke was writing. The church at the time was in the early stages of separating from the synagogue and from Judaism, as reflected by the chiding response of the ruler of the synagogue. Today's text helps us discover what it means to "claim the high ground" when it comes to the choices we must make in following Jesus, and our willingness to abandon all that keeps us from achieving our full stature of life.

Jesus makes a statement which looks beyond the Law as it relates to the Sabbath. By his actions he reminds his audience what is more important than the Sabbath and, indeed, religion in general, is that to which religion points, an almighty and loving God. He exposes how religion has become the end and not the means, a fact that is threatening to the power of the synagogue leader and every pastor, priest, rabbi, and mullah since. In contrast, Jesus reveals a God for whom the well-being of this woman is of greater importance than the law or doctrine. Matthew's Gospel records it this way, *"How much more valuable is a man than a sheep! Therefore it is lawful to do good on the Sabbath"* (12:12, NIV).

The Sabbath has its importance not as a destination, but more importantly as a direction on a journey. The Sabbath was created to serve us, not the other way around. Eugene Peterson reminds us of how worship gives us a workable structure for life; worship nurtures our need to be in relationship with God; worship centers our attention on the decisions of God. But what we do in church every Sunday is not the end result of our Christian journey, rather it points us towards our relationship with the One in whose image we have been created, one which also includes what we do for God. Are we *reflecting* God's rays of light or *collecting* God's rays of light?

The dispute between Jesus and the Pharisees over the Sabbath becomes a question as to whether the keeping of the Sabbath is more about holiness or healing. The Pharisees put the emphasis on holiness---the idea that Sabbath is a time set apart to remind us that God, not money, the boss, or the company time clock is the true sovereign of our time. But in Jesus' time holiness had come be associated with the Temple, with codes of ritual purity, and of course, with the interests of power elites. These powerful elites believed they had been put in their position to manage things, particularly including the religious elites who believed *they* were empowered to manage Sabbath keeping. Missing was the fact that it takes something more than compliance with the rules of religion to make the Sabbath holy.

The reason for the controversy is because a woman who, Luke tells us, simply "appears," has caught Jesus' attention. She had been crippled by a spirit for eighteen years. She is bent over and could not straighten up. Evident in the text is that she hasn't asked Jesus for anything. What was once an ailment has become so totally the woman's world that she no longer objects to it. Her disability has become the way she is known to others and perhaps even to herself. Jesus' call to her is a totally unanticipated summons---and yet, in the space of his one sentence, "*Woman, you are set free from your infirmity*" (v. 12), her identity is renewed. No longer is she simply a "bent-over-woman." Restored to fullness of self, this woman is able to stand straight up. By healing the stooped woman, Jesus reclaims a little bit more of creation for God.

Each one of us has a place in this story because all of us are called to this fullness of stature. We align ourselves with our favorite truths and practices, and the more closely we do so, the more they compromise our perspectives and limit the fullness of God's vision for our lives. Like the woman with the crippling spirit we bend ourselves around our convictions. Like the woman we need Jesus to suddenly show up to identify our blind spots that need correcting. We need him to show us where we need to grow in love. We need Jesus to "straighten" us out.

When we find ourselves growing impatient and itching to be unkind to somebody, Lord, straighten us out. When we find ourselves blaming the victim, Lord, straighten us out. When we find ourselves growing arrogant, Lord, straighten us out. When jealousy and pride come creeping in, Lord, straighten us out. When we find ourselves keeping a record of someone else's mistakes, and rejoicing in them, Lord, straighten us out. When we think we know it all, Lord, straighten us out. Lord, straighten us out. We are all created to throw off that which constrains us, to stand up and to strain towards God's purpose in love and praise. God does not grow old. His vision does not fail and his strength does not become stooped and bent with years.

We need stories like this to remind us that keeping the Sabbath is ultimately more about hallowing and saving life than any of the things pious folk find to argue about. Thus, in Sabbath-keeping controversies, Jesus comes down squarely on the side of the afflicted rather than the empowered. We are confronted with a

God whose movement in the world---and whose claim on our lives---is not reserved for ecclesiastically prescribed times, places, and occasions. "A funny thing happens....." on the way to the rest of our lives, and we are intercepted yet again by the reality of God-at-work in the stuff of our daily routine. The focus shifts from the God who is worthy of our response, to the people whose joy and privilege it is to respond. Inevitably, these encounters are moments of radically re-oriented grace, challenging us to pay attention---to go deeper, open wider, stand up straighter---in the recognition that all of life is lived before God.